Peter Bull's
Book of
TEDDY
BEARS

Cassell

London

For Theodore and his friends
For Bob Henderson and his friends
And that should just about cover it

CASSELL & COMPANY LIMITED
35 Red Lion Square, London WC1R 4SG
and at Sydney, Auckland, Toronto, Johannesburg
an affiliate of
Macmillan Publishing Co. Inc.,
New York

Some of the material was originally published in
Bear with Me (Hutchinson, 1969) and *The Teddy
Bear Book* (Random House, 1970)

First published 1977

Designed by Simon Bell

ISBN 0 304 29850 6

Typesetting by Art Repro Ltd.,
Printed and bound in Great Britain by
Morrison & Gibbs Ltd., Edinburgh

ii

This book is to be returned on or before the last date stamped below.

STORE

21. JUL 91

19. JUL 91

02. AUG 91

05. FEB 93

17. MAR 93

Contents

Acknowledgements

For quotations from copyright material the author is grateful for permission to include excerpts from the following in his book:

Brideshead Revisited by Evelyn Waugh (A.D. Peters)

Look Back In Anger by John Osborne (Faber and Faber Ltd)

Dear Octopus by Dodie Smith (Laurence Fitch)

Compulsion by Meyer Levin (20th Century-Fox Film Corporation)

Toys in America by Marshall and Inez McClintock (Public Affairs Press)

Summoned by Bells by John Betjeman (John Murray Publishers Limited)

The Book of the Teddy Bear by Margaret Hutchings (Mills & Boon Ltd)

The Curious Savage by John Patrick (Reprinted by permission of the author and the Dramatists Play Service, Inc)

The Enchanted Places by C.R. Milne (Eyre Methuen)

Winnie-the-Pooh and 'Teddy Bear' from *When We Were Very Young* by A.A. Milne (Methuen Children's Books Ltd)

The East Grinstead Observer

The Hanover Gazette (Mrs James Dow McCallum)

Playthings Magazine

Punch (for the Heath cartoon)

The South London News Group

The Sunday Express (The late Robert Pitman)

Which, the Magazine of the Consumers Association

Women's Wear Daily (Miss Marian McEvoy)

Personal Acknowledgements

I wish to thank the following for their invaluable contributions:
The All Saints Infant School, Upper Norwood; American Heritage; Georgina Anka; Mr Tony Bastable; Adrian Batchelor; Miss Jill Bennett; Sir John Betjeman; Sir Gangy de Brownman, Bt; Mrs Hannetta Clark; Miss Dinah Cody; One-Eyed Connolly, Esq and Mrs Helen Walton; Miss Ann Daubercies; Oliver Q. Dodger, Esq; Mr David Evans; Mrs Howard Fenton; Mrs Patricia Fitt and her family; Miss Noele Gordon; Archibald Ormsby-Gore, Esq; Mrs Howard Hamilton; Hamleys of Regent Street Ltd; Mrs Helen Henderson; Colonel Henderson; Mrs Hillier; Hunter Bunter Bear, Esq; Ms Olive Jones; Miss Sally Kovalchick; Mr Lehner, Curator of the Alpine Museum, Zermatt; Mrs Irene McBrien of Toronto; Mr Benjamin Michtom of The Ideal Toy Corporation of America; Ms Jane Miller; Ted Moore, Esq; Mr Matt Murphy; Jean Ogilivie; Hazel Pollock; Mrs Sanderson; Ann Cameron Seigal; Mr Howard Shepherd; Miss Easter Straker of Lima, Ohio; Major Stratton of the Royal Military Academy, Sandhurst; Miss Marion Waller; Mrs Werner; Mr Peter Ekin-Wood; The Worthing Museum. And above all, Mr Brian Sibley and Miss Rachel Feild, for their time, energy and loyalty.

Foreword

I have a theory regarding the buying and selling of books. It works at least as far as I am concerned. Unless you can rivet the reader's attention on the first page (and preferably also the last) – there's little chance of a sale.

The danger with this kind of book is immense, in that the very subject is so controversial. Either you like Teddy Bears or you find the entire idea of a volume devoted to them absurd and possibly involving the bringing up of bile. My main purpose is to try and persuade the unbelievers into at least a token show of interest, by offering this as a sort of 'trailer' to the contents of my book.

Did you know, for instance, that in 1906 the Tingue Manufacturing Co were using four thousand goats a week to supply wool to make Teddies? That Dame Margot Fonteyn, Lord Lambton, Mrs Enoch Powell, Elvis Presley, Sir John Betjeman and a Russian spy all have connections with the little creatures, not to mention one of the Great Train Robbers. Did you know that Christopher Robin Milne is not all that keen on Winnie the Pooh, and Theodore Roosevelt's daughter hated Teddies? (In spite of the fact that one of them has climbed the Matterhorn and another broken all speed records on land and sea.)

. . . that there are several Homes for Elderly and/or Retired Bears and that the President of a Distinguished Bank has collected over a thousand active, athletic and working bears?

. . . that a London vicar has had to exorcise a Teddy believed to be 'possessed' and that a great many children's lives have been literally saved by them? Bears I mean, not necessarily vicars. Although I'm sure they have too.

. . . That one of the most famous bears in the world is almost certainly a fake?

And now read on, gentle and fairly gentle reader.

v

1 Living in a bear world

We've been together for a decade now, Teddy Bear and I, and on one level it *does* seem a day too long. Our association tends to be exhausting and slightly claustrophobic and makes me leave undone those things which should have been done and vice versa. Scarcely a day goes by without my being forcibly reminded of my responsibilities as a confirmed arctophile or arctophilist. These two words mean 'lover of the bear' or, less emotionally, 'friend' of same.

My study of the subject began ages ago as a result of a late evening discussion among friends about childhood traumas. In the course of it, three out of five of those present admitted that their most vivid and lasting memory of their early days concerned the loss or deprivation of a Teddy Bear. I was deeply impressed by this, particularly as I was one of the three. I decided to research the whole mystique and soon found that there was enough material for at least one book.

After the publication of *Bear With Me* and its American counterpart, the subsequent material which poured in to me was so enthralling that I considered it imperative to bring the story up to date.

I cannot pretend that my book and I are entirely responsible, but it would seem that a vast Underground Teddy Bear Movement has been uncovered. I do know from letters received that the mere sight of my large aged frame carrying Teddies across a television screen has unleashed a parade of hitherto undisclosed case histories, and, even more important, rescued many a Teddy from attic, trunk or, perish the thought, a polythene bag.

This new book is meant to serve (a) as a compendium for the arctophile and (b) as a justification, if it is needed, for those agnostics who can't or won't understand what it's all about. If some of the contents are vieux chapeau to the initiated, I apologize, but the Bear Facts (such as the Beginning of It All) must not be tampered with and, in my opinion, should be restated. First I want to establish what the whole experience has meant to me personally.

Practically every post brings in some fresh problem. Often correspondents just want advice on some physical aspect of their bear (where to find a good surgeon or oculist?) and some sad people want to find a home for their old friend because they themselves can no longer accept the responsibility and/or cannot afford a major repair job. Can I help? In many cases, I'm happy to report, yes.

But I suppose the majority of the mail comes from children and older persons wanting to tell me about *their* Teddies, their idiosyncrasies, failings, virtues and, above all, their uniqueness. Snaps pour in of the bears and their owners, and we study them carefully. *We* are Theodore and myself. He's *my* special friend, in his early forties and at least 2½ inches high.

Misunderstandings abound and it appears to be common and totally inaccurate knowledge that I *collect* Teddy Bears, and, as a result I can hardly get into my London flat, let alone the small room I keep on in New York, now it would seem entirely for their benefit. A direct and, to some people, distasteful follow-up to all this was my appearance on the front page of the *Radio Times,* in bed or rather on the bed (so that there will be no misunderstanding) with Mr Fyfe Robertson and a lot of bears. This was for a programme called 'Collector's Corner' if I remember correctly. A collector of bears I am not. But I have had bears thrust upon me and the brutal truth is that I'm at heart a one Teddy Man, for to me the actual possession of a Teddy is an immensely personal thing and it seems natural to prefer one above all.

Later on you will read of people who have hundreds, nay (I love nay, don't you? It means 'yes' in Greek rather surprisingly) in one case thousands of bears. Well, one thousand anyhow. But I think your extreme loyalties belong to a particular one and, though I have several whose qualities are such that I have a certain affection for them, ordinary Teddies, acquired from shops, not as gifts or bequests, are unable to rouse a great deal of interest in me. Show me a bear, however, who has been loved, beaten up, deprived of limb, eyesight or hearing and I am instantly intrigued and want to discover his history.

Every time I return to my flat of an evening I am reminded of my weakness, because I am faced on entry by a collection of seemingly neglected and accusing glum furred faces. Yet I only have to see a bear lying in or near a dustbin to rescue it immediately, germs and all, from such an ignominious and totally undeserved fate. Though why *I* should worry about this particular problem is ludicrous, as I only have to find the Royal Borough of Kensington and Chelsea refuse van Number JAM 900M for the refugee to be swung off the ground and attached to the front of the vehicle. For the remainder of his life he can have a lovely time whizzing through the two swinging boroughs.

I think there are several vehicles of this type which are Teddy-orientated, and I wonder how many ex-owners recognize their loyal but deserted friends. A short time ago a theatre-manager friend of mine wanted a Teddy to use in a play he was putting on at the Fortune Theatre, called *The Tiger and the Lady*. He had in mind an old-fashioned bear, but he did warn me that the actor chosen for the role would be thrown about a bit. I asked my little lot for volunteers and, except for one, they turned down the job flat. But Dusty said he wouldn't mind as long as he got full credit in the programme. (Dusty was one of the afore-mentioned drop-outs or should I say throw-outs?)

Unfortunately the show was not a a great success but Dusty got a goodish review in *The Times,* which he now wears attached to his wrist with a throw-away of the play. The other bears are now regretting their decision and there is a movement afoot for me to ask the proprietors of the *Spotlight* Casting Directory if they would introduce a special section for aspiring Teddy artistes.

Near the Notting Hill Gate end of Kensington Church Street there is (or was) a window full of the creatures, watching the world go by. I was curious about their rather sedentary life and finally had the impertinence to ring the front-door bell on some pretext or other. 'Oh,' said a charming lady, 'they used to belong to my children but somehow they got left behind when they left home. I expect they'll want them one day and meanwhile the bears are just waiting to be fetched.'

And while we are in that area of London, you only have to walk round the corner to find Zodiac, *the* Astrological Emporium, an enterprise of which I am a partner. I don't think I would ever have undertaken this had there not been a Teddy Bear sitting on the floor of what was then the owners' sitting room but is now the Office, the Mailing Dept and the waiting-room for the Clairvoyant's clients. The property was advertised in the *Evening Standard* and there were a lot of people after it, as it was freehold and in spiffing nick. I was just about to leave for New York so a snap decision had to be made. My partner Mr Busby, an arctophile, and even the lady who was selling 3 Kensington Mall seemed keen. We all looked at Teddy and he nodded his head so we said 'Snap'.

The fact remains that one is Teddy Bear conscious in the same way other people are car, garden, tits, clothes, food or cat conscious. I want to make this book a personal one, describing the effect and influence that Teddy had exerted over the man, woman and child in the street. Or the home, come to think of it. I didn't want to do it analytically, by searching for hidden meanings and digging about in people's minds. I want particularly to avoid case-history reportage as much as poss. This would make the whole thing heavy-handed and the bears would hate it. Imagine their faces when told they were labelled Case Number a hundred and something.

But every day there is some reference to a Teddy either in the Press or on television. Headline-stealers the little dears are and no mistake. I liked very much the recent divorce case in Dusseldorf, where a Teddy was one of the chief witnesses.

Willi Mayer, a wealthy industrialist, suspected that his wife was having it off with his chief accountant on a skiing holiday in Switzerland. So he sent in a spy, a cuddly Teddy with a bouquet of red roses and a loving letter. In the bear's ear, unknown to *him* of course, was a device which picked up not only every sound from Frau Mayer's bedroom but a reference to the eighty thousand marks which she had withdrawn from her husband's account.

It will be recalled that a bugging device of a similar nature was attached to a bear belonging to that Mrs Levy who pulled poor Lord Lambton through some lurid mud. Teddies are always being taken advantage of, poor innocent animals, and not very long ago in a notorious 'sex and bribes' trial, a Mr Maurice Cochrane, the Managing Director of a big company under investigation, was reported as having 'sat cuddling a huge Teddy Bear to which he occasionally referred for advice, when he interviewed three prospective salesmen'. On the other hand, Mr Cochrane did spare the bear the indignity of appearing as a witness for the defence.

And what about the remarkable case of the evil Teddy Bear who had to be exorcised? The ceremony was performed by the Rev David Wickert at a flat in Wimbledon, of all places.

Two girl students were convinced that there were wicked influences at work, when they heard heavy breathing — not emanating from themselves — in the flat they shared. Seemingly the sounds came from a Teddy belonging to one of the girls. The owner suddenly remembered that a strange incident had occurred when she was a little girl in Africa. One of the servants in Ghana had taken the bear and slit a hole in his left wrist. 'I later discovered,' said the girl, 'that breaking a limb is a voodoo ritual to enable a spirit to enter a body.' When Linda, for that was the girl's name, moved into the new flat, she took the bear out of storage. A few days later the phenomenon of the breathing started.

Mr Wickert, Vicar of St Andrews Church, Wimbledon, was not unnaturally a tidge sceptical at first, but when he saw the genuine fear of the girls, he realized it was not a joke. He placed a palm, which was shaped like a cross and had been blessed in church, in the girl's flat and prayed for the evil spirit to leave the bear.

'I was told later,' he said, 'that the people downstairs had heard banging throughout the time I was in the flat. As if the spirit was being cornered.'

Linda remarked, 'I am convinced the spirit left the bear and our flat that night.'

The Reverend Wickert rather surprisingly held on to the bear and stored it in a spare room at the vicarage. 'I haven't heard a sound from it,' he reported, 'but I'm keeping it away from my three children.'

4

So, kiddies, if you hear heavy breathing in the south western area of London, you will know where it probably comes from.

But that's enough about Naughty Bears. Let's get on to the usual run of Good Bears. What could be more typical of their real nature than this recent item of newsprint?

'I was seven and on holiday with my parents in Brighton. I was carrying my Teddy as I paddled. Suddenly a wave took me by surprise and I dropped him. He was swept out into water too deep for me and I shouted "Save him!"

'A boy swam a few strokes to Teddy and brought him to me. My hero! The rescue led to our parents meeting and they became friends so I saw quite a lot of my Teddy rescuer. We now have two little girls but they don't have my Teddy. He's my treasure.'

A gentleman who also owes his wife to a Teddy Bear is a Mr David White. He was asked to a party and met a young lady called Claire Emmett. (He had been invited in mistake for another Mr D. White, incidentally.) Some time later Miss Emmett gave him a T. Bear, which prompted Mr White to ask him if he should marry her. The bear said yes he should, and he did, and I should jolly well hope they are all living happily ever after and raising a small family of Teddy Bears.

It is of course a great help if an arctophile finds a marriage partner, who, if not one themselves, at least understands the position. Recently a young lady got a wonderful surprise at her wedding when her much-loved Teddy turned up at the reception in a special suit made by her mother. Her husband, in responding to the toast, mentioned him as part of the family, as was only right and proper.

With almost monotonous regularity somebody rushes to the defence of the Teddy Bear, as if his very existence were threatened, apart from his integrity. In the staid old *Times* the heading 'The Twilight of the Teddy Bear' not surprisingly caught my eye. Underneath there was an angry letter from a Mrs Louden of Liverpool accusing Mr Marvin Glass of 'Talking Through His Hat' about Teddy Bears and Raggedy Ann Dolls being superseded.

'Children need some personal object on which to vent their anger,' quoth Mrs L. 'Had he' (the unfortunate Mr Glass) 'tried to knock the living daylights out of one of his sophisticated toys? The Teddy and the rag doll will come through many such ordeals and still be loved and usable, but not so an expensive walking-talking doll.'

Mrs Louden is absolutely right. The great advantage of a loyal friend who can't answer back is that he can assume any guilt or blame without fear of denial. 'Teddy did it' is a phrase which must have passed thousands of tiny lips, when a valuable piece of Ming has been swept to the floor or a door slammed in somebody's face. I know a young gentleman from Boston, Mass, who went on using his bear as a shield for his iniquities for so long that his parents finally sent him to a psychiatrist.

We arctophiles are a touchy lot and insults or ridiculing by ignorant persons

5

puts our hackles up (can that be right?) and in order thoroughly to mix my metaphors (though carefully to avoid splitting an infinitive) it's fair to say that we are up in the saddle before you can say 'knife', with our lances poised to launch a counter-attack.

Since the publication of the original book and the subsequent bearhaha, I have learned how vulnerable one had to become to contempt, abuse, disbelief, admiration, bull-baiting, sarcasm, flattery and opportunities to cash in on the whole thing.

It is a bit worrying to realize, from the point of view of integrity, how enormously the Teds have contributed to my career, to say nothing of my financial betterment. They form the centrepiece of so many of my enterprises. The Ladies' Luncheon Clubs, which I bang on at, expect Theodore and at least two other bears to put in a personal appearance. When I do 'An Evening of Bull' round the Universities of America and anywhere else they will have me, the entertainment (if so it can be entitled) opens on a bare and dark stage with a single spotlight shining down on a chair in which sits my Senior Teddy (a rising seventy-one).

I leave him there until the very end of the evening, giving no explanation for his presence, and I sometimes think he is the only factor which keeps the audience in their seats. I don't provide the latter with an interval as I daren't let them escape from the theatre, hall or auditorium, in case they disappear into the night saying, 'We can't go back. It's only that fat man. No one else is coming on.' So I carry on yacking, acting, overacting and finally I turn to Teddy and say, 'Now it's up to you.' And he never lets me down. The moment interest is focused on him, a wave of bonhomie sweeps through the place and before we pack it in, the audience are telling us about their teddies. I haven't so far dared to inflict 'An Evening of Bull' on British audiences, but, if I do, I shall have to rely heavily on Theodore and his friends to pull me through.

His friends (*Best:* Schoolgirls and bears always have at least three Best Friends) are Crotchety, H.H. and Tiny. Crotchety was crocheted (it's all right. I looked it up in the *Pocket Oxford*) by the grandmother of a friend of mine, Cynthia Lindsay, the American writer, about seventy years ago and he's still in remarkable shape, albeit he is only just over an inch high.

H.H. was sent me directly after a TV appearance of Theodore and myself in the States. He arrived pretty anonymously in an aluminium soapbox accompanied by a short note, just signed with the two initials. It appeared that H.H., as I immediately baptised him, had reposed in a lady's sewing-basket for forty years or so. He had been given to her by someone she loved, who had died. She decided, on viewing Theodore on the small screen, that he would make an ideal friend for her small companion, and that anyhow a change of scene was advisable. H.H. has only one ear but he is very musical and sits at his piano for

1 A hug of bears

2 Dusty the actor

3 Mr Frost, Sir John Betjeman and Snowy in conference

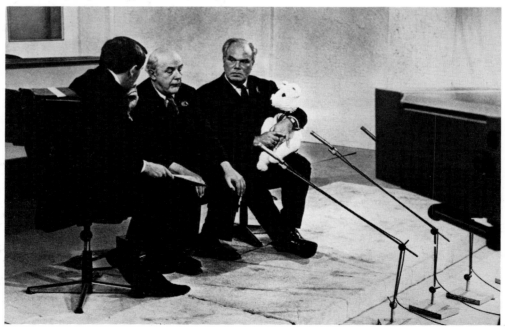

4 Not to be thrown away with the rubbish

5 & 6 Mrs Henry Hamilton and her wedding attendants

hours, bashing away at his Bach. Theodore is enormously impressed and brings him light refreshment from time to time (Beer for Bach, Lemonade for Liszt) but refuses to Turn Over.

Tiny was made for me specially by a lady schoolteacher and I've been wont to tell all and sundry that he is the Tiniest Teddy in the World. He is beautifully made and shows up ever so nice in the palm of my hand in close-up. But I am seriously considering giving up my claim about him as it can lead to trouble.

I was sitting at the counter of my shop, minding my own business and not doing very much of same, when an individual appeared from nowhere in front of me and went into the attack at once. I have to point out that a few days previously I had appeared on 'Nationwide' with Tiny and bragged.

'I've got the smallest Teddy Bear in the World,' the gent announced, and produced a minute plastic creature which didn't look much like a Teddy to me (although on third thoughts he did resemble a miniature Martian one).

He was, he said, just off to enter it in the *Guiness Book of Records.* 'Goodness!' I found myself exclaiming. He handed me a card with the animal's measurements on it. With a slight feeling of nausea I noted that the pupils of the eyes were 0.005 and that, if standing, it was 0.375 high. It didn't say 0.375 what though. Please note that this is the only occasion when I use the word 'it' to refer to a Teddy Bear. If you could have seen 'it' I'm sure you would agree with the classification. Anyhow I decided not to contest the issue as I thought it would be disagreeable for my small Tiny to have to stand up against the wall and measure *his* height. So I just said 'Jolly Good Luck' to the gent and went on polishing the silver.

The joke of it all is that a few weeks after this incident a lady who had organized a Teddy Bear fiesta in Bexley, Kent, sent me the most exquisite Teddy, far smaller than the 0.375 high one, who makes Tiny look like a giant. Sadly he is so small that he has to live in a box to avoid my rather haphazard light dusting.

Mark you, if one is prepared to bare one's soul and indeed heart to an object which is for many no more than a 'stuffed toy', one must expect to meet a certain amount of resistance, and in many cases a sort of brick-wall lack of understanding or even any desire to communicate about the subject on any sort of level.

Take the television chat shows for instance. I have learned in a hard school to be prepared for any contingency, and I rather look forward now to a prejudiced or just plain ignorant interviewer. When I was doing a promotion tour for the book in the States I sometimes did as many as twelve shows a day on radio and TV combined. Occasionally the host would lead with his chin and I would catch a glimpse of my work beside him, not even taken out of its cellophane wrapper.

'I'm afraid I haven't had time to look at your book yet,' mine host would remark cheerfully but unwisely. It's rather like Mr Finney saying to the waiting

National Theatre audience (and I'm making no cracks about that building just in case...), 'I'm afraid I haven't had time to look at the script of *Tamburlaine* but I'm going to have a bash.' Well, not quite like that but you know what I mean. Anyhow I'd reach across for the book, take the wrapping off and say with a delightfully disarming but lethal smile, 'Well, you've got a little time to look at it now, while I tell the viewers or listeners all about it and how I came to write it in the first place.'

There was another type of unwary interviewer who would leap in at the deep end. The sort of question he or she would open fire with would be: 'Don't you think it a bit childish to collect Teddy Bears?'

'I don't think so,' I would reply suavely, and you've no idea how suave I can be. Funny how the word 'suave' seems to have passed out of our vocabulary. When did *you* last meet someone who could be described as suave? I would continue, 'Childish? No more childish than collecting wives, cars or yachts.' And then I would go in for the kill.

'After all,' I would go on, 'Teddies don't do any harm. In fact, quite the reverse. Look at the spheres they've excelled in. They've climbed the Matterhorn. When did you last reach the top of a famous mountain? They've broken every speed record on land or sea, at least Donald Campbell and Mr Woppit did. Have *you* broken any speed records lately? And they have saved lives. There are numerous cases of children being brought back to life, just through the *feel* of a loved Teddy.' Unless I really *hated* the interviewer I didn't go as far as asking him if he had saved any children's lives in the past year, but by this time I was usually in command of the situation and could get on with the serious job of flogging the book. A lot of the above, now I come to look at it, is pure fantasy but it's what I *should* have said and now believe I did.

But I did have all my facts marshalled in my head and was just waiting for somebody to demand case histories. Actually one was so recent and given so much publicity that it is possible you remember it. It concerned a small boy called Mark Wallis who was knocked down by a car and rendered unconscious. Day by day he lay in a semi-coma in a hospital bed, unable even to recognize his parents, who feared that his injuries might prevent him from ever regaining full consciousness.

Then Mrs Wallis had the brilliant idea of taking him his favourite toy, a Teddy Bear which she placed gently beside him. This provoked an instant reaction, and the familiar touch and feel of his friend awoke something in the child and led to a remarkably swift recovery.

And here's another sobering news story which was oddly moving. When that poor boy was murdered by drowning at the lido on Hampstead Heath, his friends sent to the funeral of the fifteen-year-old Enrico Sidoli a Teddy Bear wreath of white chrysanthemums inscribed to 'Our friend Enrico'.

12

But now I'm afraid it's back to me. The American tour was full of droll incidents. Obviously travelling with a Hug of Bears is not likely entirely to pass unnoticed. The Senior Bears have their own luggage marked T. Bear Esq. Theodore always superintends the arrangements. The principal item is a very large Gladstone-type but Revelation-made case. The bears hate being shut in and it is possible to leave the zip open so that their heads are free to see what's going on, and at the earliest opportunity they are released from their semi-captivity.

The plane journeys are full of fun. I seat the senior and larger Teddies on a vacant seat (funny how those Jumbos so often aren't full!). Then before take-off I ask a passing air hostess to help them fasten their seat belts, please. The girls' reactions vary. One gaped at me and them in terror, and dashed off to tell the captain. It was reported to me afterwards that she had informed him that there was a suspicious-looking fat gentleman on board who might be a hi-jacker and what's more, the little creatures sitting beside him might very easily have firearms concealed about their persons. The captain apparently roared with laughter and later the attention the bears got was almost embarrassing, though they loved every moment of it. Trays full of honey, comics and toys were brought to them constantly during the flight.

On the ground the Teddies present problems when on tour, though oddly enough they whizz through Customs as if they had Diplomatic Immunity. This in spite of the fact that, not so long ago, a large Teddy was found lying on a bench in Rio de Janeiro airport, containing just the five hundred and twelve pairs of nylon panties and two hundred and ten dresses. I am sorry to say that, in this connection, their bodies have been used for smuggling not only jewels but dope as well. In America the power of television is such that it usually ensures us a nice welcome. But the studios themselves can make things difficult. For some of the very early shows (over there it's not unusual to be 'on' at 6.30 in the morning) the authorities want me to leave the bears overnight but I tell them that this is out of the question.

In theory I suppose, I should insure the dear old things, but this wouldn't really compensate for their loss, and imagine the internal jealousy it might stir up if they found out what they were valued at. Here perhaps is the appropriate moment to submit a cast list of some of the other characters in my own company of players. Four and a half of the Smaller Set you have already been introduced to.

Other notable personalities include Delicatessen, the one who was left on a shelf in a Maine grocery store for fifty years by Miss Euphemia Ladd. He is particularly hump-backed but who wouldn't be in the circs? On her retirement Miss Ladd sent him along.

Of almost equal seniority is 'Fishy' who arrived at the stage door of the Ethel Barrymore Theatre, where I was falling out of a rocking-chair twice nightly in

Peter Shaffer's highly risible *Black Comedy*. Fishy was sent me by a lady from Florida who was, she said, 'finding him too much of a responsibility'. He was huge and endearing, but when opening the enormous paper parcel in my dressing-room, I noticed a really horrible smell emanating from his feet. I investigated further and found at the bottom of the wrapping a packet of by now rotten fish fillets sent from a local store. The package had been franked and stamped and the whole affair seemed quite incomprehensible. I wrote to all the authorities concerned to complain that things had come to a pretty pass in a so-called democratic country, when one couldn't even send a Teddy Bear through the post without attaching denizens of the deep to his poor feet. I did eventually deduce by process of elimination that the fish had slithered in by error, when the Florida postal authorities were checking or rechecking the original parcel, suspecting a bomb or something. Fishy, or Stevie as he was né, now sits merry as a grig in the flat of Sally Kovalchick, one of the most distinguished editors in New York.

Then there's Brownie, one of the only Greek-born bears I have met. I think it must be something to do with the hot climate and subsequent effect on fur, but few Mediterranean countries are Teddy-orientated. Brownie is or was of Royal descent and belonged to one of the Greek Princesses, who always summered in Corfu when she was a little girl. She had an English Nanny, always a strong supporter of the Teddy Bear movement in the early days of Teds and the later days of English Nannies.

I have a very dear friend, Marie Aspioti, who, though Greek, speaks English rather better than I and certainly has a larger vocabulary. She was often invited to partake of Royal teas at Mon Repos, where incidentally Prince Philip was born, if you know what I mean. Marie, then a little girl, gazed with longing at the T. Bear and, when she left the Palace, the Greek Princess gave her Teddy to Marie Aspioti who gave him to me.

The only other Greek bear I know is called Rufaco and he still belongs to a ravishing Paxiot (a native of the island on which I have a dwelling), called 'Eftihia', which means 'Happiness'. Quite a name to live up to but I can assure you that she comes through the challenge with flying colours. A few years ago she married a young Englishman called Bill Hobdell, who brought as part of *his* dowry a biggish bear called Bibi. The couple and the two bears are inseparable and a delightful quartet they make. The only discordant incident I can remember was when the car was being packed for a journey to England. Owing to lack of space Mr H. wanted to put the bears in the boot. A tremendous row ensued, won, I am happy to report, by Eftihia.

'No! No! No!' she shouted, 'they must be able to *see*! *Everything!*' she added. So they were put facing the back window of the car. Some fairly laughable incidents occurred on their odyssey. There was a splendid drama at the French

14

frontier when the Customs official, after letting the car through, rushed after it. He made them stop and, pointing at the bears, said it was illegal to bring in dogs without a permit. Rufaco and Bibi are, I understand, instructing their lawyers to sue the French government for libel and in ursine circles are confidently expected to win.

Not unnaturally there is a strong theatrical flavour about some of my bears. Quite apart from the well-known actor Dusty, already referred to, I have the Teddy Bear from the original production of *Hair*, given to me by a member of the original cast of that extraordinary entertainment, the late and extremely gifted Jonathan Kramer. Then there are the friends given to me by stars, which will, I fear expose me to the accusation of bear-dropping. There is a quite exquisite hand-painted number, of great softness like his donor, Anouk Aimée, who once (and I'm being a Filthy Sneak) bought a Teddy for her daughter and then kept him.

Then there's Tab, who has a suede back and a crocheted front, made by Mr Hunter himself, a real labour of love. He admitted that he found the paws dodgy to do and so young Tab is holding a small bouquet of flowers to hide any inadequacy of limb. Joan Greenwood gave me two tiny china friends, perfectly jointed and of simple delicacy, in little knitted dresses which I have never dared wash. They tend to be musical and sit at H.H.'s feet and turn the whole thing into a sort of Musical Afternoon.

There are Sheridan, Annabel, and Wilton, three priceless solid silver Teddies, disguised as receptacles for what is now never called the cruet. They are named after the children of their father, the donor, Robert Morley, who has now been one of my closest friends for just the forty odd years. And goodness some of them *have* been odd.

A fresh arrival to the family is A.M., given to me be the delectable Ann-Margret, who played Lady Booby, to my Sir Thomas, in the recent film *Joseph Andrews*. Although in the movie she leaves me to drown in the Roman Baths at Bath without a qualm, while she and Miss Beryl Reid are busy lusting after young Joseph Andrews (the wildly gifted Peter Firth) my dear new friend has A.M. imprinted on his bow for all the world to see. The other bears are more than a little jealous and I can see that I shall have to find a star with the initials P.M. to present me with a companion for him. Patrick McNee, par example. Do Avengers have Teddy Bears? That's what I ask myself.

Let's get on to the next chapter, for heaven's sake, and tell the reader how it was In the Beginning.

In the Beginning there was...Please Turn Over.

2 In the beginning

I must confess that at the start of my research I had no idea that America claimed the Teddy Bear as its own discovery, and I suppose I was hoping against hope that while I was in the States I would stumble on some new evidence to prove that this was not the case. I knew there was a very small school of thought (British to the core) that maintained the toy was so called after a visit of King Edward VII, then Prince of Wales, to the London Zoo. He took, it is affirmed, a fancy to a Koala Bear, and who should blame him?

I did get involved in a certain amount of correspondence supporting this theory. A Mr Kirby of Little Rock advised me to look at page 5422 of Funk and Wagnall's *Standard Reference Encyclopaedia,* where I would find that 'the Koala somewhat resembles the toy Teddy Bear which was modelled after it'. I took Mr Kirby's statement on trust as I had already found on page 4194 of the *World Book Encyclopaedia* (1953 edition) that 'the Koala is a small Australian animal that is also called the Teddy Bear'.

But there are two *principal* contestants for the honour of having made the first Teddy. They are Morris Michtom, who later founded the Ideal Toy Corporation of America, and Margarete Steiff of the German firm of Steiff. There has been great bitterness between the two over the years, and there is still a good deal of mystery lurking round the foundations of both their claims.

What *can* be established without the shadow of a doubt is that the whole thing was sparked off by a distinguished cartoonist of the period called Clifford Berryman. For it was he, while working for the *Washington Star,* who drew a picture of Theodore Roosevelt refusing to shoot a small bear cub on a hunting expedition in Mississippi in November 1902.

16

Roosevelt, the youngest man ever to serve as President, had succeeded the assassinated McKinley in 1901, and a year later had gone south to settle a minor boundary between Mississippi and its neighbour Louisiana by drawing a line between the states. Berryman, in his simple but historic cartoon, shows the President, gun in hand, turning his back on the small bear and holding up his hand to indicate that he was indeed 'Drawing the Line in Mississippi', as the sketch was entitled – a *double entendre* to indicate that he could not bring himself to shoot such a small sitting target.

Berryman's work appeared in newspapers and magazines all over the continent, but I doubt if he realized what an astonishing effect this particular creation would have on the world. The little bear was to become a kind of symbolic signature to many of his political cartoons and provide the President with an endearing and valuable tag which could be (and was) used constantly for publicity purposes.

Somebody who did see the possibilities of the little bear was Morris Michtom, a Russian immigrant. He was the proprietor of a small candy store in Brooklyn which also sold toys, many of them handmade by him or his wife. The moment he saw the drawing he had a brilliant idea. He and his wife cut out the shape of a brown plush bear and stuffed it. The animal had movable limbs and button eyes.

Mr Michtom put one in the window of his shop, alongside a copy of the Berryman cartoon, and attached a label saying 'Teddy's Bear'. It was sold almost immediately and replaced by another, and so it went on. Mr M. began to suspect he was on to something good. But did he need authorization from the President of the United States to use his name to promote the article?

Eventually he screwed up enough courage to enclose a sample of the bear with a personal letter he wrote to Mr Roosevelt, whose Christian name the little bear was destined to carry to immortality. In due course he received a reply from the White House in the President's own handwriting, saying that he couldn't imagine what good his name would be in the stuffed-animal business but that Mr Michtom was welcome to use it. In those days it was not possible to patent a trade name, a factor which accounts for the later rush of 'Teddy Bears' from everywhere imaginable.

The enterprising Mr Michtom went ahead with his plan and took the Presidential letter to a Mr Schoonmaker, the buyer for Butler Brothers, a large wholesale firm dealing with toys and novelties. In 1903 this firm took his entire output of Teddy Bears and guaranteed his credit with the local mills which supplied him with the actual plush to construct the animals. Today the Ideal Toy Corporation is among the biggest manufacturers of toys in America. But in those days there was no real hint of the furore the Teddy Bear was going to cause throughout the world, although by the time Mr Michtom was fully established, there were dozens of firms turning out the little animal all over America and

17

Europe (Sears, Roebuck is believed to have been handling them as early as 1904 and Woolworth's in 1905).

The other main claimant to the invention is the firm of Steiff in Germany, founded in the 1880s by Margarete Steiff, a lady fated by polio to spend most of her life in a wheel-chair. Margarete and her sister possessed the first hand-driven sewing machine, which they used to set up back to front so Margarete could turn the wheel with her left hand, which was also somewhat crippled. Yet this remarkable lady was determined to be financially free and independent.

In 1877, when she was thirty, she got very interested in the use of felt, which was then a comparative newcomer to the field of dressmaking. One day by chance she found a model of an elephant, and as an experiment, made one out of felt. This she turned into a pin-cushion and kept for herself. Her friends were so delighted by it that she made some for them. In 1880 there were six in existence; by 1885 there were five hundred and ninety-six; and the next year, five thousand and sixty-six. In 1886 a monkey was added, followed by a donkey, horse, pig and camel. In 1893 an agent sold her toys for the first time at the famous fair in Leipzig and a catalogue was brought out.

By this time two of her nephews had joined the firm and one of them, Richard, conceived the idea of making a toy bear. This animal had always been his favourite at the zoo, and he used to spend a great deal of his time in front of the cages and artificial caves in which they were housed. His aunt, it is reported, was not enthusiastic when she saw the toy; firstly, because she thought it was too large to be popular, and secondly, because it was made of mohair, which was difficult to get in those days.

Later, seeing a bear with jointed limbs and made of plush, she thought something could be done with it. The firm decided to have a try and sent one of the bears to Paul Steiff, another nephew, who was at that time undergoing vocational training in America. He tried to interest various American business-men in them, but they apparently ridiculed the poor creatures for their plumpness, heaviness and general nonconformity.

All this is particularly curious because it was during this year that Mr Michtom was, it seems, having his success, on however small a scale, in his Brooklyn store with the animal. The Steiff model, with adjustments, was exhibited at the Leipzig fair in 1903. The buyer of one of the biggest New York import houses took a great fancy to it. I suspect it was F.A. & O. Schwarz, but most of their old records have been destroyed and it is impossible to prove this.

Anyhow, the representative of whatever firm it was approached the Steiff people, saying that he hadn't been able to find anything new and worthwhile at the fair and that he was looking for something 'soft and cuddly'. The bear was produced and the buyer put in an order for three thousand immediately. Serious manufacture at Steiff started in 1904 and the bear appeared in the Leipzig catalogue in 1905. The great selling point at this time was that the bear was a boy's toy and a perfect foil for the doll.

It is around this time that the Steiff story gets merged inextricably with supposition. It is reasonable to think that there can have been no question of the animal being called 'Teddy', because the word would have meant less than nothing to the average German. It is also fairly certain that he was known as 'Friend Petz' until quite a good time later, except in America.

Of course the other Steiff animals were also enjoying an enormous success, and by the time Margarete Steiff died in 1909, her brain-children had become famous all over the world, with 'Knopf im Ohr' (button in ear) as a trademark for her merchandise. You see, other German firms had been cashing in, and in 1907, for instance, the toymakers of Sonnenberg in the Thuringian Mountains were shipping ten thousand bears to America every week.

The Michtom claim to invention is certainly a strong one, though here we run into a series of seemingly inexplicable loose ends. There is, for instance, no trace of the three essential letters which would prove for all time that Morris Michtom was Teddy Bear's originator.

One is his letter to the President, which understandably was not filed in the White House at the time, but Theodore Roosevelt's reply, giving his permission to use the name of 'Teddy', is another kettle of fish altogether. It seems extraordinary that such a valuable document has not been preserved and treasured through the years. Its impact for publicity purposes would have been dynamite, and its display (even in photostat form) on the walls of the New York office of the Ideal Toy Corporation would impress every buyer in the world.

Later there was a letter from Mrs Theodore Roosevelt to the younger Michtoms to condole with them on the death of their distinguished father, who was mourned in the newspapers throughout America as 'The Father of the Teddy Bear'. But neither letter has turned up, though Benjamin Michtom remains quite sincerely convinced that his father did indeed invent the 'Teddy Bear'.

Well, there you are. Take your pick. I am always accused of running with the hare and hunting with the hounds. While I am inclined to support the Michtom story, I also think it highly probable that the Steiffs had brought out a species of 'Teddy' at the same time, if not before. But I bet the Russians were manufacturing toy replicas of their national animal centuries before *either* of them.

Let's just admit that whether it was a he or a she, an American, a German, a Russian, or an Englishman who first caught the magic in his hand, children and grownups of all ages the world over owe him an awful lot.

Immune to all the controversy it had unwittingly stirred up, Berryman's Teddy Bear continued to appear for many years. In October 1907, another

DRAWING THE LINE IN MISSISSIPPI

BIRTH OF THE TEDDY BEAR (1902)
The tubby cub supplanted wooly lambs.

8 Senior citizen American
bear

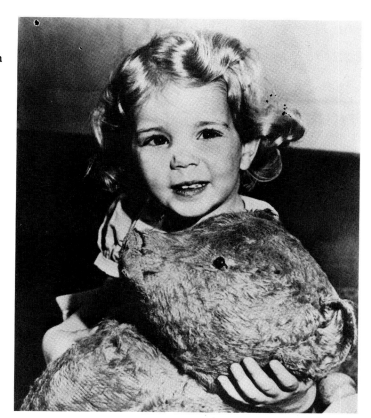

9 An original Steiff

Presidential bear hunt was the inspiration for another very successful drawing. Called 'The President Dreams of a Successful Hunt' it shows him with one foot resting on a dead bear (BAD TRUSTS). Tied to his waist by a belt marked RESTRAINT is another bear, live but cowering (GOOD TRUSTS). In the background is the original Teddy Bear, happy as a sandbear, carrying a sackful of bears.

The symbol was still being used in 1917, when on the eve of America entering World War I, Mr Berryman drew a cartoon of which there is no trace of publication. On the back of the original drawing is written: 'Given to my father John Paul Ernest'. It shows the President of the United States (Woodrow Wilson) with one of his hands clutching a scroll titled 'Strenuous American Policy' and the other grasping Uncle Sam, who is sitting gloomily at a desk, surrounded by lurid posters saying things like 'Hun Atrocities in Belgium', 'Lusitania Sinking' and 'Red Cross Hospitals Attacked by German Airmen'. Uncle Sam is protesting, 'I fear I've waited too long', but Wilson, firm behind his pince-nez, says, 'It's NEVER too late to start RIGHT.' In the background Teddy Bear stands coyly but bravely holding the American flag.

Although Teddy was appearing in print from 1902 in the form of drawings, he doesn't appear to have crashed any other medium. In May 1906, the first advertisement for Teddy Bears seems to have been presented to the general public. This was in the toy trade magazine *Playthings* and read: 'This is Bruin's Day . . . The American line of jointed plush bears is the real thing. Polar Bear, Cinnamon Bear, Grizzly Bear. Baker and Bigler sole manufacturers.' Note that there is still no mention of the magic word 'Teddy' though the patriotic emphasis in the ad suggests that foreign bears had already seriously invaded the market.

In 1906 Kahn and Mossbacher, manufacturers of dolls' outfits, were urging customers to 'make our happiest hit your happiest hit! Everything for the Teddy Boy and Teddy Girl!' Ferguson, an early toy pioneer, offered Teddy in a baseball suit, a turtle-necked sweater, overalls and even Rough Rider uniform. The Keystone Novelty Company was willing to sell 'Bears fully equal to the finest imported' — which again shows that the home producers were determined to lead in the bear market.

A manufacturer called E.J. Horsman appears to have been the first actually to *call* his bears 'Teddies' when advertising his wares in *Playthings*. In fact, he put 'Teddy's' which he amended to 'Teddy Bears' in November 1906 when offering the latest way of using the animals, in the form of side lamps for cars. He was obviously not all that patriotic, as we find him in December 1906 pushing 'Imported Teddy Bears — best quality with voice $4.50 to $70 a dozen — and also DOMESTIC TEDDY BEARS with voice, Horsman's extra quality $9 to $36 a dozen'.

Although the craze for Teddy Bears greatly increased the sale of all kinds of stuffed animals, there is no doubt that it was only the Presidentially-inspired toy that caused so much fierce competition among toymakers and stores alike.

The Tingue Manufacturing Company of Seymour, Connecticut, was apparently using the wool of four thousand goats per week. These animals were now immensely valuable: a good buck (if I may use the phrase) fetched as much as a thousand ditto.

1907 saw the creation of the Bruin Manufacturing Company. The Fast Black Skirt Company rather surprisingly turned out 'Electric Bright-Eye Teddy Bears — Shake the Right Paw, Eyes Light Up White or Red. Also Thirty-six-inch Bear with Autos'. Leo Schlesinger offered Teddy Bear pails and Teddy Bear tea sets, while the Lloyd Manufacturing Company of Menominee, Michigan, announced: 'The Best Selling Novelty of the Year', which turned out to be Teddy Bear carts and cages. Pedal cars were advertised with bears driving them; a Teddy Bear hammock was followed by a Teddy Bear squeeze ball; there were Teddy Bear targets, paper dolls, party games, penny banks, blocks, wagons, scarf pins, rubber stamps, water pistols, postcards, candy boxes, cotillion favours, ballons, bags, briefcases (of plush, natch!), books, card games, shooflies, rocking horses, muzzles, and leashes. Strauss, the self-designated 'Toy King', made a 'self-whistling Teddy Bear'. There were Tumbling Teddies and even one with a doll's face, which seems about as far as you can go.

Certainly the whole thing was going *too* far for some people. There was, for instance, a Michigan priest who denounced the Teddy Bear as destroying all instincts of motherhood and leading to race suicide. A Mrs Harry Hastings of New York answered this by saying: 'Nonsense! I think they are the cutest, dearest, best-behaved little visitors we've ever entertained. I draw the line on their going to church, however.'

There were other replies to the irate clergyman. A baby-carriage merchant announced that 'Teddy Bears may be a menace to motherhood in Michigan but we are selling more baby barouches than ever before!' And a woman on Sullivan Street in New York gathered ten of her fifteen children around her and said (and I quote the newspaper verbatim):

'Tiddy Bears, is it? An' sure more than half the kiddies on the block have thim little growlers, an' I don't see any signs av race Soorside in this neighborhood. Oi think that afther wan or two more come along to give me a noice dacint family to bring up, Oi'll be gittin' Danny to git me a noice big Tiddy to kape in the house.'

Many people worried over another aspect of the craze: the decline in the popularity of dolls. A poem, published in a magazine called *St Nicholas*, was entitled 'The Days of Long Ago' and was written by a minor poet of the period (I use the word 'minor' in its strictest sense, for Miss Marion Lincoln Hussey, the author, was only nine years old at the time):

In the long ago I was once brand new,

With silk and satin and lace.
My coat was of velvet, my hat of real felt,
And oh, I moved with such grace.

After a few more lines of boastful reminiscence by this allegedly lovely doll, the poem ends:

But no, oh, 'tis said that I am disgraced
By a modern Teddy Bear.

'It is enough to make a perfect lady of a doll mad,' a magazine editor wrote. 'The dear little girls, who have always cried for dolls at Christmas, are this year crying for Teddy Bears, and dolls are left on the shelf to cry the paint off their pretty cheeks because of the neglect.'

And *still* some toy people would not believe the craze would last. In October of 1907 one retailer claimed, without a sign of a wink, that 'Bears are on their last legs'. A month later, however, he had to admit 'that crazy bear is as popular as ever'.

And indeed he spread to all fields. The circus at Madison Square dressed some of its clowns and even performing dogs as Teddy Bears. And in certain vaudeville shows of the day the chorus girls came out dressed as them. In the 'New Operatic Absurdity' called *The Toymakers*, there was a song entitled 'There's Nothing Else But Teddy', in which a Miss Grace Lavelle was accompanied by four young ladies, hideously disguised in bear costumes that must have been stifling.

Then there was the popular joke of the period: 'If Theodore is President of the United States with his clothes on, what is he with his clothes off?' Answer: 'Teddy Bare'. The joke had a British counterpart as well: Lily Langtry, the Jersey Lily and King Edward VII's great and good friend, was said to prefer her Teddy Bare. But the Teddy Bear craze was never as frenzied in Great Britain as in the States, where between 1907 and 1911, everyone was positively Teddy Bear mad. In Minneapolis, the Dayton Dry Goods Company had a 'Live Teddy Bear' to welcome the children every afternoon at four-thirty. One of the big stores in Philadelphia, for the opening of the baseball season, had a window display of the ballpark with Teddy Bears in the uniforms of the Athletics and Phillies, in which grandstand and bleachers were full of cheering bears. In one clothing emporium, Teddies were dressed in really gorgeous gowns of velvet and lace. And wearing jewels. Lawks! Luckily, to balance things out, other bears wore Columbia, Yale, and Princeton football uniforms and carried footballs.

Then there is the legendary story of the blue-ribbon bulldog (worth $2,000 according to its New Orleans owner) which had been brought up with a bear cub which, alas, died suddenly. The dog lost its spirit, its appetite, and finally even its desire to live. One day, on the way to the vet, the dog saw a Teddy Bear in a window, approximately the same size and colour as his old friend. Pressing his nose against the pane, he refused to trot on. His owner bought the Teddy Bear

24

and the bulldog regained his spirit, put on weight, and loved life once more. He carried the Teddy tenderly in his mouth wherever he went, poked the bear's nose in his dish of food at mealtimes, and slept on top of him at night (which I can't think was wildly comfortable for poor Teddy).

The craze was at its height in 1909, when Theodore Roosevelt left the Presidency. Since that hunting expedition in Mississippi, where the whole thing had started, he had served out three years of McKinley's second term and four of his own. He had busted trusts, started digging the Panama Canal and mediated in the Russo-Japanese war: yet to millions he will be known best for his participation in the birth of the Teddy Bear.

And what of the original animal, made with such perspicacity by the candy-store owner in Brooklyn, Morris Michtom? As late as June 19, 1963, there is a letter (fortunately extant) to Benjamin Michtom from Mrs Kermit Roosevelt, saying that her children still didn't want to part with it, but in fact he now rests in the Smithsonian Institution. Theodore Roosevelt's great-grandchild was photographed with the original Teddy (in person) on the sixtieth anniversary of his birth.

Right at the end of this book I may very easily make a sensational revelation on this subject, but I'll trouble youse readers not to cheat and have a peek.

What I do have to report now is the memory of a delightful visit to Washington to see Mrs Alice Longworth Roosevelt shortly after the publication of my book. During her lifetime she was a, if not *the,* leader of Capitol Society and even in her middle eighties a remarkably active and informed lady. By devious means I managed to get hold of her phone number and, to my amazement, she herself answered the blower. I told her that I wanted to bring her a copy of my book and when would it be convenient for her to receive me?

She gave me a date and time and told me that under no circumstances was I to bring anybody from the Press or any Teddy Bears! I must say I viewed my approaching visit with some trepidation but I needn't have worried. On arrival at the large house in Pennsylvania Avenue, I was put at my ease by a young relative of Mrs Longworth's, who had just come back from Corfu and knew at any rate of my existence. On the stroke of four my hostess made a wonderful Ethel Barrymore-like appearance and a real English tea was served by a butler, with muffins in a heated dish and one of those giant silver teapots with a hot water jug to match.

The great lady was extraordinarily candid but witty with it and told me her father never possessed a Teddy as far as she knew. What had happened to the one Mrs Michtom had sent him she did not know. She did however admit that he was not at all averse to using the bear and his connection with him for electioneering purposes and political propaganda.

But it became clear that Mrs Longworth was not prepared to talk indefinitely on the subject and soon she was launched on a series of hilarious reminiscences of her trips to Britain, including a visit in her teens to attend King Edward VII's funeral.

Eventually I took my leave and have to confess that I was only five minutes out of the house before I was closeted with my friend Richard Coe of the *Washington Post*. This meeting took place in a bearby hotel, and though the results in that newspaper were not perhaps quite so sensational as the Watergate affair (emanating from the same source), we did make the front page. Theodore Roosevelt's daughter, Theodore (whom I carefully hid in my pocket), and I.

Children of today can't believe that the toy is only seventy-five years old or that it hasn't been around for ever. But as you will see from the following pages, Teddy's appeal for young and old has never faltered, and though he is younger, he is just as stable an institution as Father Christmas. And, I fancy, just as indestructible.

3 Here, bear and everywhere

     One of the more surprising phenomena I have unearthed in the vast, seemingly underground, Teddy Bear movement is the number of sensible, witty and totally together collectors of the animals, who have written to me since they learned of my interest in the subject. If the bear dens in America seemingly outstrip their European counterparts, you must remember that there is more room over there for housing the dear little things, though I have heard of cases of Squatters in Camberwell.

But take Matt Murphy for instance, the Present of the Californian branch of the Bank of Montreal. He has just moved for the third time in five years to a house which had two special features to attract him. A sumptuous kitchen for his wife, Medora, and a den on the third floor which had ample shelf space and room for his thousand bears.

Now it must be admitted that these are not all *Teddy* bears because Matt collects bears period. In an impeccable inventory he lists their construction and countries of origin. There are fifteen gold, twenty silver and thirteen ivory bears for starters. Only one hundred and ninety are made out of wood, but, under the heading 'Miscellaneous' we find leather, walrus tusk, pipe cleaner, rubber, soap, cork, straw, chocolate, sponge, whalebone and mastodon tusk (natch). A small Teddy from Korea sits beside three guitar-playing bears from Russia. Paraguay, the Philippines and even Iceland have added to Mr Murphy's treasure trove.

But his real heart is undoubtedly in his proper Teddy Bears ('Large, Medium, Small and Miniature: 193' as they are entered in this astonishing catalogue) and his pride and joy are two American Football teams who play each other throughout the season. On another page you can see one and I'm here to tell you

27

that, on a fairly recent trip to England on business, Matt brought me some of his star performers to take a gander at. Travelling in a tremendously smart briefcase, they were an impressive sight.

In his last letter he spoke with pride of these athletes' achievements. 'With six seasons of fourteen games each of football now completed, some of the bears have built awesome records of performance over the 84 games played. Some highlights:

'Bear No 13, as Quarterback, has completed 1,069 passes of 2,002 passes thrown for 16,411 yards and 99 touchdowns.

'Bear No 1, as Tight End' (Goodness, I sometimes think that the American language is more difficult than the Greek one) 'has kicked 84 field goals (252 points), 216 conversions (216 points) and caught 36 touchdown passes (216 points) for the 684 point total.'

Matt sent a sensational series of photographs and one of them was of four of the bears about to engage in some lawn tennis. 'As you'll note,' writes Mr Murphy with quiet pride, 'No 13 is not only a stellar Quarterback/Passer in football, but a good Tennis Player.'

Several ardent arctophiles have built houses for their bears. A lovely lady called Dinah Cody has just such a house and she entertained us both right royally when we visited her in Chicago while promoting the American edition. Dinah, who has taught ballet dancing and belly dancing in her time, is a photographer of great talent and I had already received a preview of her bear house. But both Theodore and I were totally unprepared for the welcome we got. They were all living at that time in a huge second-floor flat (to the Americans for some reason the second floor is always rated as the third floor) just outside the city in an area known as Hyde Park.

We entered the building and saw to our amazement bears forming serried ranks up the two flights of stairs as a Welcoming Committee. They were holding banners and both British and American flags. Slogans like 'Theodore for President' and 'Mr Bull for Mayor' were hoisted aloft, and on arrival at the actual flat there was a huge concourse of bears, all of whom had left their snug house to greet us. We were greatly touched by the whole thing and Theodore was so overcome that he readily accepted an invitation to have a nice lie-down in the spare room in the Bear House, where a bed had already been turned down for him.

I studied the edifice with great interest and realized that they were still in their Summer Quarters because, on top of their spacious apartment, there were deck chairs, lilos, parasols, a barbecue around a miniature swimming pool, complete with water and diving board. A few years ago Dinah's sweet mother died and there was a Move which the bears didn't take to all that kindly. Theodore got a fairly frenetic letter from Head Bear.

28

'We don't know what's going on here but whatever it is we don't like it. Everything is topsy-turvy and this makes us nervous. The big Teddies don't like it either and they have to live right out there in the midst of the uproar. At least we still have our house. *She* says "not for long". What do you think *she* means? Please advise.'

They are now, I am happy to report, comfortably settled in a huge room where I visited them fairly recently. Dinah and her Aunt Ruth come over to England frequently and Theodore is on the receiving end of some very thoughtful presents. A stocking-cap arrived, 'to keep the cold away from *one* ear anyway as it fits best over only one'. And a pair of dark glasses to wear skiing in the winter, on the beach in summer and when the spotlights are too glaring during 'An Evening of Bull and Theodore'.

Another happy association I formed (if only in correspondence) was with an entirely bear-oriented family called Fitt. Well not entirely b.o. because as Patricia Fitt pointed out in an early letter, 'My husband is a fine broadminded human being with absolutely no interest whatever in bears. I am sadly certain he is the type who doesn't even *see* them if you know what I mean. I just asked him if he ever had a Teddy Bear and he said he couldn't remember and I had better ask his mother. You see what I mean.

'In my cloudly infancy I had a Teddy about 7″ tall, white fur and much loved. He vanished and I don't remember anything about it but still have somewhere the newspaper advertisement seeking his return.

'I was given a substitute Teddy, who is at this moment sitting on a chair, crutch by his side, in our basement workshop. My Teddy story follows so many of your reports. He was always with me and certainly when I had my appendix out at fifteen. He has, since my marriage, stood patiently in a shaving mug, leaning on his cane. He has a walking cast, having broken his leg thirty years ago. My father, who was chief sewer-on and darner at midnight, put on the cast and made the crutch after deciding the threads or more darns would not have anything solid to hold on to. Teddy has also had to look at the events of my life unfold with his one good eye.

'Number One Child was a doll lover though she did have two other Teddies of mine (about 18″ high, one white and one brown). *I* did play with them but they got lost or abducted or something.

'Number Two Child slept with his own Teddy for a number of years until he inherited Number One's Mousey and he slept with Mousey until he got ashamed. His Teddy and Mousey are in a box in the basement until he gets a wife.

'Number Three really started the whole thing seriously. Ann (for that was her name) had a great friend called Antonia Palfrey, who happens to be Theodore Roosevelt's great-granddaughter. The two girls were great pickers of dustbins.

One day they found two wooden liquor boxes (one from Messrs J. Walker) and lugged them home,. They put partitions in the cases and moved the bears in, The kids were about nine at the time. The bears were originally in cardboard boxes, with Kleenex for sheets, but quickly became more sophisticated. These, now called the Patriarchs, were little 3" Steiff bears. My son Craig was constantly trying to horn in on the activities but was generally loftily excluded but slowly (mainly because adults kept saying "Don't be mean to Craig") he became a part of the bear goings-on. I don't think he ever had his own wooden box but he may have. I know lots of his allowance went into subsistence for the bears. All this was real playing. Books were written, mythologies were created, past history discussed and bear personalities firmly established. There was a lot of arguing and discord but the Bear House kept thriving.'

Catie, the eldest daughter, took time off from college and went to the Corcoran School of Art where she spent a year making pottery. The bears benefited because she made them a wonderful stoneware bath tub which is so big that they have to bathe with the 'share a bath' system. They use a ladder to get into the tub, incidentally. Catie also worked a few hours a day at Skender's Greek Import Store, which imported olive oil in wonderful boxes.

When the Fitts moved to their present New Haven house, they were accompanied by forty-seven Greek olive-oil boxes, fully furnished, with forty-nine bears, one cat, three rabbits and two mice. The Bear House takes up one end of the Fitt dining-room and is stacked seven storeys (boxes) high. There is a school-room where a Social Studies book is kept which is always getting lost and, Mrs Fitt hopes, always turning up again. It dates from the very early bear days in the Fitt household, days of Indian Ink and tiny pens. The author was Hist Orian and inside the cover it said 'Molasses Bear. Please Return'. There was also a text-book called 'Spelling for Fun. Ha. Ha.'

The Bear House is a respectable commune. There are no female bears, though there are baby bears. Living with them is Miss Armour who has been their housekeeper for years. She is (and I quote Patricia Fitt), 'a dowdy warm-hearted rather silly mouse and has her own room with a brass bed and a portrait of her mother. Reepicheep, another but male mouse, comes and goes but does not live there as far as I know. He doesn't *seem* to work for the bears.'

Early in our correspondence Patricia broke the news to me that Miss Armour had fallen in love with Theodore and was knitting him a scarf. Later dispatches showed a slackening in romantic interest: 'The confusion in our land has got even Miss Armour distracted and her knitting of T's scarf has slowed down. Partly because it is rationalized that he won't need it until the autumn and partly because it has been suggested that she looks like one of those old crones sitting on the tumbrils (no one in this house is *quite* sure what a tumbril is) during the French Revolution. I think the accusation is way off, for I fear deep down she is for Agnew Bear. That is a cruel thing to say but she's certainly a law and order type, at least in the Bear House.'

Finally, months later, the bottom dropped out of the Scarf for Theodore market. Miss Armour threw it away because she had dropped so many stitches out of nerves, the lady from *Life* magazine never returned the pictures of the Bear House which little George and Craig had sent her and, as a final chapter to a saga of mishaps, Dido Twite, an English Siamese, kept trying to destroy the whole organization of the Bear House by kidnapping some of the inhabitants and taking them under the sofa to beat them up.

But to go back to a description of the original construction of the Fitt Bear House. One of the principal contributors was young Craig who, at the age of eleven, was given a power saw. That and the presence of a 'wonderful toy store' near the house made the task for Craig and Ann (to say nothing of Mrs Fitt herself) easier. As the latter points out, in a shortish time the bears had everything they wanted.

The following separate establishments were put into operation: Little George's General Store. The Blue Marlin Restaurant. The Hostel. The Theatre (complete with Prop Room and Scenery Dock). Buddhist Temple and A Chapel of All Faiths (note: new organ needed). Workshop. Art Studio. Young Children's Playroom. Nursery. Fisherman's Shack and Dock. School Room. Post Office. Butcher's Shop. Little Kids' Room. Laundry. Children's Dining-Room and Adults' Ditto. Three to four living-rooms, including a Music Room complete with Bazouki kit. Numerous bedrooms, two bathrooms (one with Catie's bathtub). This also has a very grand throne toilet complete with chain-pull and a crown painted on it. The little bears tend to fall into the latter, it is reported from well-informed circles.

But perhaps the star attraction of this remarkable building is the Art Gallery and there are some marvellous family portraits in it. A sea captain bear with a telescope in his hand and a clipper in the background. He's all done up in a nautical suit, complete with brass buttons. There's an archaeologist bear in pith helmet and carrying some bones. Then there is the rich ancestor who left all the money to enable his successors to live in such luxury. Florence Nightingale Bear is the only woman in this portrait gallery. There is, however, I am happy to report, a photograph of Mrs Fitt's own Teddy who really Started It All and also a picture of George Washington, who is the only human being to grace the collection.

Finally, I would like to list some of the names of the denizens of the Bear House, because they indicate the sheer inventiveness and wit of the entire enterprise. Cinquefoil Bear. Simon Barsinister. Mischief Owl. Brouhaha. Wasi-Wuki. Bernard Leach. Dirk Ure Lion (because, it was kindly explained to me, he wears a hairpiece).

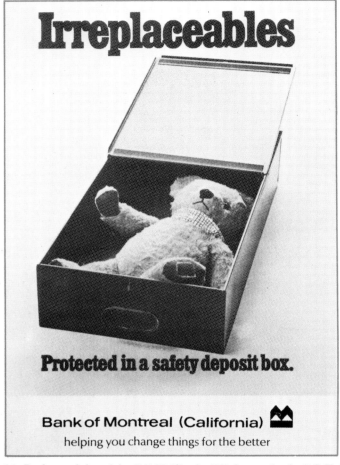

Irreplaceables

Protected in a safety deposit box.

Bank of Montreal (California)

helping you change things for the better

11 *Back row, left to right:* (12) Halfback, (13) Quarterback, (15) Fullback, (10) Flankerback. *Front row, left to right:* (1) Tight End, (11) Right Tackle, (14) Right Guard, (2) Center, (30) Left Guard, (3) Left Tackle, (6) Split End

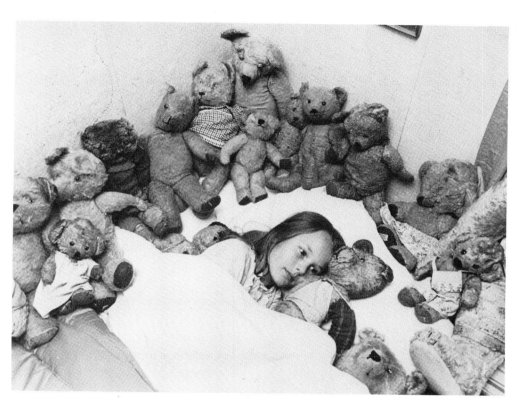

I must add an extremely sad postscript to the above which I feel should be included, though it may diminish the delightful effect of the Saga of the Fitt house. In 1976 the marriage broke up and the bears now lodge (for reasons of space) on top of Mr Fitt's garage in Washington. But in the spring of 1975 the Bears had their day of glory, being on exhibit in New Haven and attracting hordes of people, young and old, and 'generally showing off'.

Despite her troubles, Patricia Fitt retains her astonishing sense of humour and her last letter started off: 'The Bears and I have been on hard times and it took various postmen this long to get your letter to me. My swan song was a Bear House pottery which was/is pretty smashing. I fear to ask you about the Colonel who started the Bears in the World Thing because I resented females being Bearesses so didn't join. Our bears are more enlightened than that!'

Which brings us to the Colonel in person, the doyen of the entire Teddy Bear movement in Europe. Without him I doubt if I could ever have ventured on one book, let alone two, dealing with the subject. He has supplied me with an enormous amount of material, to say nothing of ammunition with which to pound the cynics. His name is Bob Henderson and he is President of the unofficial Teddy Bear Club. He is also one of the two instigators of a very worthwhile charity organization, the Good Bears of the World, details of which can be found at the back of this book.

He possesses a small army of around four hundred bears, a unique collection. Besides a great many of the popular type in every size, he has Teddies in the shape of money-boxes, teapots, cruet sets, candles, paperweights, chessmen, matchboxes, brooches, castings, tobacco jars, shoes, puppets, and even umbrella stands.

He is especially proud of his 1903 Teddy, a 'Mark *One* model' as he calls him. This animal, who is two years older than his owner, started life as the property of his elder brother, and then was shared by the two boys. Later he was inherited by the Colonel's daughter, Cynthia, and changed his sex. Cynthia insisted on dressing him in a frilly skirt and so he became a Teddy Girl.

During the war Colonel Henderson carried a miniature bear as a mascot who accompanied him wherever he went. Throughout the North West European campaign they served together on General Montgomery's staff.

It was the Colonel who put the whole thing pretty lucidly in a description of the Teddy Bear Club's raison d'être and aims:

'The Teddy Bear Club exists universally in the subconscious plane of the mind. From time to time, however, it comes into conscious existence at various places all over the world. All those who have an affection for Teddy Bears and their lovers, who appreciate the value of the teddy as an instrument in psychotherapy, and in this way are teddy-bear conscious, are automatically members, though at first they may not realize it.

'Through this appreciation a teddy bear can bring together two, or more, complete strangers. In this way new friends are made and many pleasures can be shared. Goodwill can be spread abroad and the Teddy Bear can be described as a truly international figure that is both non-sectarian and non-partisan and functions as a powerful instrument of goodwill.'

Recently Colonel Henderson had a letter from a lady asking if she could have one of the small bears from his collection. He sent her one, faintly surprised by her request, and got a letter of thanks. The lady explained that she had been very lonely but found that if she carried a little Teddy Bear in her handbag, she had only to produce it and someone would start a conversation.

'You see,' she wrote, 'I am blind.'

Colonel Henderson is from Scotland as is young Deirdre Mackinnon, whose collection is well into three figures. The notable thing about her little lot is the large percentage who have been found abandoned, or rescued from rubbish bins, etc. Floppy was picked up from a shop ownerless, Cocoa was sitting forlorn outside Deirdre's front gate and Og was saved from a rubbish tip.

New names for Teddies always fascinate and an American lady from New Hampshire has supplied me with a splendid range. She inherited her first bear in 1911 from an elder sister who didn't care for him, but Dorothy Green did. He was her constant companion for many years and slept with her every night until she went to college. When she returned years later, complete with husband and son, to live in her parents' house, she found him still there. She had three more children and then one day she found Teddy was a sight only a mother could love. She didn't want him laughed at or played with so roughly that he would disintegrate, so, in what she thinks must have been an evil moment, she wrapped him up tenderly, patched paws, stuffingless body and all, and cremated him.

About thirty years elapsed before Mrs Green got mixed up with Teddy Bears again, and this is the unusual part of the story. Some ten years ago she was exploring the rooms of a four-storey junk shop and, 'I found a lovely Teddy sitting alone in a shabby old armchair looking wistful, forlorn and pinched in an unheated room. I couldn't resist. I bought him and he became the first of my new family of bears.'

He was christened Ursus Major and was followed smartly by Secundus, who was found in a basket of supposed rubbish at a flea market, costing fifty cents. Mrs Green operated on him successfully a number of times and he is now golden-brown, rejuvenated and at least eight inches tall. Peregrina (née Peregrine) was a gift from a college mate. Mrs Green tried to make him a velvet suit but the trousers simply wouldn't work out. So she made 'him' a skirt and changed his sex. Peregrina is now a chic and sprightly 65.

Minimus is the smallest bear but as he is several inches taller than my Theodore, I am keeping mousey quiet about his actual height. Mrs Green is mayhap the most erudite of all arctophiles and her next bear was called Quondam Caecus (formerly blind, as if you didn't *know*). He is 'a mean-looking bear and not at all cuddly. When he was given me he had hard flat buttons for eyes that made him look sightless. I painted some pupils on his bone eyes but he still has rather a mean look.'

Eboracum is a blonde bear about five inches high, so called because, as Mrs Green so helpfully explains, 'Eboracum is the Latin for York', whence he came, saw, and conquered, I imagine.

Minimissimus is aware that his name is bad Latin but he was smaller than Minimus and given to Mrs G. by an 82-year-old woman. Ecclesia was given to her by another elderly lady (yes, *her* name *was* Church), and is the spitting image of Mrs Green's deceased Teddy, therefore dearly loved.

Borealis, so called because he looks almost like a polar bear, was originally very blonde (now an off-grey, Mrs Green admits). Her eldest daughter says he looks very snobbish as if he were thinking, '*I* am a bear, who do you think you are?' Her son bought him for Mrs Green at a jumble sale where some heartless owner had put him on the slave block.

Amabillissimus (very loving) was sitting on a table in a junk shop and when Mrs Green asked the proprietor how much the bear was, he said, 'That dirty old thing? Oh, a quarter, I guess.'

'You never saw a quicker sale.' observes the new owner. Cassius Rufus, her newest acquisition, is a deep mahogany red. He had no eyes, but the resourceful lady has improvised some from four black pins and two black buttons. Don't ask me how!

'Sine Pedibus (without feet) is our cripple. His arms were intact and moved very nicely on joints when I got him. But he never had any legs, so he sits all day in a little cup filled with tiny pebbles and peers out over the rim very appealingly.'

There are several other bears in the Green collection, but Mrs Dorothy gave the new one to one of her sons-in-law, who though 'otherwise a normal young man' was also an arctophile. So he has acquired Albus (white), Gratis (free. I shouldn't have put that in. Any fool knows that one!), Patruelis Australia (southern cousin), and one or two others. Mrs Green rather surprisingly had no idea that 'anyone else felt as I did about bears. I was pleased and reassured that many find comfort and pleasure in the dear creatures.'

In a PS she told me that not only were her husband and four children very indulgent of her whim but that one daughter had asked that she would will her bears to her.

A lady whose entire family understands the whole mystique is Mrs Werner, whose daughter owns the bear from another planet, about whom you can read in Chapter 12. She (Mrs W.) was born in Berlin and at the age of 2½ was presented

36

with a lanky, skinny yellow bear whom she named 'Jomi Mitschki'. He became instantly the focal point of her young existence. As she explains, she had to experience all sorts of nasty rejections, as a little Jewish girl growing up in the Hitler years. But Jomi and her wonderful Papa contributed hugely to what happy memories she has of a pretty tricky childhood. Her father used to take her for leisurely strolls in the Tiergarten of an evening, Jomi dangling between them on both shabby paws. 'And many was the time we greeted a gentleman also out for an evening walk, who turned out to be Albert Einstein. I am of course convinced that he tipped his hat and smiled at my Teddy.' (I wonder if Mrs Werner knows that Dusty Springfield has a greatly loved Teddy called Mister Einstein.)

Anyhow, Jomi was very fond of beer apparently, and usually appeared in the mornings quite intoxicated, singing little bar-room ditties. Mrs Werner's father died when she was ten years old and Jomi became increasingly indispensable. Particularly after the war started and he had to share the air-raid shelter with her. In the spring of 1941, 'I demanded something awful of him,' wrote Mrs Werner. 'He had to abandon his Fatherland and come with me to the United States.'

In 1946 everything took a turn for the better and Mrs Werner acquired a wonderful husband and had two children in the fullness of time. Jomi stayed with them but, alas, time had aged him by then and the manipulations of a little boy proved too much for the old gent. He passed on, leaving a number of descendants. One of these was Bunga-Dingalung who is still with the Werners and sleeps with them, eats with them and visited Europe with them in 1971.

Mrs Werner, now a grandmother, has sixty-five bears and several of them are of very high lineage or distinction. They include Ernst Ludwig, the Grand Duke of Hesse-Darmstadt (Bearer of the Iron Cross), and Getzo Hashimoto, godson of the Empress Nagako of Japan who sewed him out of Imperial throne covering. He is at present the East Asian authority at the Museum of Ober-Ramstadt in West Germany. The remainder come from all over the world, some picked out of the gutter and lovingly restored.

Finally, there was a Miss Elizabeth Bentley who has over a hundred bears, ranging from a two-and-a-half-inch one in a pink sweater to Lord Neville who is four feet high. She was married recently to Mr Howard Hamilton, and the cake at the reception was decorated with two Steiff Teddy Bears dressed in full wedding regalia. Now the whole lovely blooming lot live at the delightfully named 'Jumping Branch' in Virginia.

Boss asked 'Teddy' for advice at interview

MAURICE COCHRANE, 51, the former managing director accused in the "sex and bribes" trial, sat cuddling a huge teddy bear, which he occasionally referred to for advice, when he interviewed three prospective salesmen, Glasgow Sheriffs' Court was told yesterday.

The episode was described by ROBERT THORBURN, 68, former rotary salesman, of Dalry Road, West Kilbride, who was giving evidence on the 19th day of the trial.

Hugging a teddy bear or any other stuffed animal may sound like kid stuff but a growing number of adults are resorting to this practice to cope with tensions or feelings of insecurity.

This is the opinion of two psychiatrists who told The ENQUIRER that people love to own, caress and display stuffed toys because it gives them a feeling of comfort they cannot get from pets or other people.

One psychiatrist, Dr. Jean B. Rosenbaum of Santa Fe, N. Mex., president of the New Mexico Psychoanalytic Assn., even contends that the teddy bear represents a substitute sex symbol, especially in cases of deprived individuals.

For example: "A woman who lacks a man has to have something to cuddle. So she will hold a teddy bear, which is a lot easier to handle and doesn't create any of the frustrations that come from dealing with another human being."

Dr. Irving Markowitz, director of the Child Guidance Clinic in East Orange, N.J., says present day stresses are such that adults are turning to stuffed toys to relieve a sense of helplessness over their own troubles and the world's ills.

REVOLT OF THE PADDINGTON BEAR STUFFERS

Angry women get sack
in Teddy factory row

FUR flew when eight women teddy-stuffers got in a paddy about cuddly Paddington Bear.

They said they would not work with

Paddington Bear . . . centre of the dispute

'Find my Yellow Ted' pleads toddler

A SPECIAL "missing person" report was issued in Havering this week — by a heartbroken toddler.

Three-year-old John Biscoe lost his dearest friend—a small, battered Teddy bear—during a shopping trip to Hornchurch and Romford last Monday.

EXORCISED..

AN EVIL TEDDY BEAR!

ONLY the terror in the voices of two girl students persuaded a vicar to pit his powers against the forces of voodoo.

Please, they begged . . . break the curse of the evil teddy-bear.

And he did. By clasping the two-feet-tall cuddly toy — there it is on the right — and **EXORCISING IT.**

The weird ceremony was conducted by the Rev David Wickert at a flat in Wimbledon, South London.

Last week he said: " I seriously believe the teddy might well have been possessed by some sort of evil spirit. "

The terror began when music student Linda de Winter heard heavy breathing in the flat. " It was horrible. The breathing was slow and rhythmical, but rasping, too." she said.

" And the sound always came from the teddy-bear."

Strange

Flat-mate

Kids love Fred the teddy bear

F RED is a cuddly teddy bear who'll give you a bright and friendly wink if you talk to him.

He is the latest toy in Staffordshire's homes for deaf children.

He looks like any other teddy, but under his golden fur he's a marvel of electronic gadgetry.

A tiny microphone in his head picks up the sound of children talking to him and relays the sound through transistorised circuits in his body.

Yellow lights behind his eyes glow brighter or dimmer according to the pitch and volume of the baby talk Fred hears.

Helpful

The 16-inch tall teddy is an adaption of a well-used idea. And in his short life he's proved very helpful in teaching deaf children to talk.

These children have to learn how to vary the pitch and pronounce syllables properly.

Until Fred was constructed, about a fortnight ago, the method was slow and boring. The children watched a needle jump about on a dial as they spoke.

But the lights in Fred's eyes are more fascinating and understandable.

Toy shop

Fred came from an ordinary toy shop before the people in Staffordshire Education Authority's audio-visual department did some surgery on him.

Mr Brian Greenwood, a field service engineer who looks after all the maintenance of the department's audio-visual teaching aids, said, " It was the idea of Miss Kennerley, one of the teachers.

" In one case a little girl who couldn't make any sort of sound had quite a conversation with Fred when she'd only known him five minutes."

The department hope to develop other ideas for older children along the lines of Fred.

Man's best friend is his teddy, says the colonel

" A MAN'S best friend is not his dog — but a teddy bear." I was sitting in the lounge of Lt.-Col. Thomas R. Henderson's home in Braid Road, Edinburgh. Around me were about 30 of Colonel Henderson's collection of 100 bears.

There were bears of all sizes—bears used for

4 If you go down to the woods today

You are not in for a big but a *huge* surprise. Almost any woods as a matter of fact, for the great Teddy Bear Revolution is in full swing. All over the world small groups are springing up to celebrate and cement the legend of the little chap named after Theodore Roosevelt. Ever heard of a small village in Norfolk called Brundall (pop: 2,574)? Well, in 1970 there was a Carnival there and the object was to raise funds for the local Memorial Hall. Some enterprising person suggested that a Teddy Bear competition might be an attraction.

Prizes were to be given to the happiest, the saddest, the smallest, the tallest, the scruffiest and the prettiest Teddy Bear. It seemed a modest project but a miracle happened, and it turned out to be the biggest Teddy Bear Picnic ever. Between twelve and fifteen hundred turned up, of all colours, shapes, sizes, growls and creeds, and were eventually put on display, and three thousand people turned up to see them.

'Brundall has never seen anything like it,' said Mr T.I. Gates, the secretary of the Hall Committee. After the main prize-winning Teddy Bears had received their awards, it was a question of scraping the pots, in the form of a thousand mini-jars of honey given to the first thousand entrants by Reckitt & Colman. Incidentally the Carnival raised £600.

Statistics are, I know, apt to be boring in bulk but I must dish out a few more to prove my point about the Upsurge of the Teddy Liberation Front.

In 1970, two thousand students attended a giant lunch-time Teddy Bears' Picnic in the grounds of a former Government House in Auckland, New Zealand. In the next year five hundred popped along for a competition held in

40

Edinburgh, Scotland. In 1972, two hundred T. Bears were collected and presented to the Royal Hospital for Sick Children in Glasgow. In 1973 they had a 'Hug of Bears' at Macclesfield (six hundred present) and Coventry replied in 1974 with three hundred furred guests. In 1975 another big picnic took place in Edinburgh (a census put the figure at six hundred or more).

Most of these festivities were in aid of some charity or other, and it has now been proved that the Teddy Bear is one of the most powerful fund-raising instruments you can find. Little did the first one think he'd become a symbol of good-doing and benevolence.

Special organizations have now been set up all over the place and the Wessex Teddy Bear Association plans regular festivals. The first one was held in June 1975 and Mrs Boniface, its prime mover, sent me the glad news of its success. Three hundred and forty-five bears in various classes of distinction turned up and had to face television cameras and interviewers galore from steam radio. On the forthcoming agenda of the Association are the gift of bears for hospitals and a Special Fete, at which there will be a Teddy stall, devoted to Teddy sweets, gingerbread cakes, pens, handkerchiefs, aprons and home-made Teddies.

The ingenuity of these fiestas never ceases to astonish me and I particularly liked some of the original classes in which the contestants at the Coventry gala could be entered. The fattest, the friendliest, the best-dressed and the 'most curious' were among the qualities to be assessed, and it is the last which intrigues me most. Did the good people of Coventry mean the most inquisitive or the most eccentric? I suspect the latter because we know, from the incident of Lady Godiva, that the people of this city can be extremely uninquisitive. Suffice to point out that one of the competitors belonged to the Area Medical Officer and another to the Chief Superintendent of Police.

In the Chinese Astrology Calendar you probably know that the years are divided up into animals, viz: the Year of the Snake, the Boar, The Rabbit, the Rat, etc. Actually, 1976 was the Year of the Dragon but will be best remembered by arctophiles as the Year of the Bear. The fiftieth birthday of perhaps the most famous of all Teddies, namely Winnie the Pooh, was celebrated in October of that year and details of the shennanigans will be found in the chapter devoted to this illustrious bear.

I fear I wasn't able to get out to Oregon State University, where a unique Festival took place in October and was to last at least six weeks. Its special feature was 'Teddies and Trains', an original combination to say the least. It was staged in the Horner Museum and the Curator very flatteringly invited Theodore to act as one of the judges in the numerous competitions. Arctophiles from all over the States were invited to submit entrants and I sent Fishy along from my New York collection.

It being Bicentennial Year, red, white and blue bears were sold who, I blush to report, chanted the Declaration of Independence if their batteries were working properly.

The overwhelming and enduring popularity of the Teddy Bear (probably only surpassed around 1910) has led to a lot of awkward but not unfunny incidents. Take for instance the affair known as the 'Great Teddy Bear Caper' at the Crocker National Bank in California. In order to whip up trade, the promotion department came up with a seemingly stunning idea, 'Sunny the Bear'. The deal was that anyone who opened a new checking account of three hundred dollars or more would be given a bear.

'It started out great,' reported Angela Bohning, then the new accounts girl at the Palos Verdes branch of the bank, 'but then problems began to arise.

'There were bears sitting on the counter as cute as could be and everyone wanted one. Customers who already had accounts insisted they should get a bear. One man who had a fifty thousand dollar account threatened to take out his whole deposit unless he got a bear. We tried to tell him and others just to withdraw three hundred dollars and open another account and some of them did. But mothers would come in with two or more kids and each child wanted a bear of course. But it was one account, one bear, so they had to open two or three checking accounts.'

On top of everything a bear shortage began to develop. The top brass sent down word that there must be strict accounting for each bear.

'It got so at our branch that we had a bear account at the end of business every day,' recalled Mrs Bohning. 'The tellers had to balance their bears before they balanced their drawers. We finally had to appoint one of the assistant managers as "bear man"! He would count them and then lock them up in the vaults at nights.'

As the bear shortage grew worse, various branches of the Crocker Bank tried to wheedle more Sunnies from others which still had a reserve and the Palos Verdes branch sent a pickup truck to an office in Orange County. There are rumours it carried an armed guard. Finally Crocker ran out of bears some time early in 1976 but it was weeks before the outcry subsided.

'I remember one woman marching in with a teddy bear she had bought at a department store,' said Mrs Bohning. 'Her son would have nothing to do with it because it didn't look like Sunny. She wanted to trade it in for a Crocker bear but all those had gone by then.'

In all one hundred thousand Sunnies went to bank customers. David Sanson, a spokesman for the bank, said that although it might try other promotions, 'we will never come up with anything like the bear'.

The Crocker Bank had posters showing a dear little Teddy in a striped vest with the words 'Free – with Love from Crocker Bank'.

Incidentally Matt Murph's outfit, the Bank of Montreal, has a smashing advertisement for safe deposit boxes, illustrated by a Teddy lying snugly in one, with the slogan 'What to Do With Your Valuables'.

In Great Britain it is calculated that sales of Teddy Bears account for eighty per cent of the soft toy industry and forty per cent of these are bought by grown-ups for grown-ups, but I'm not convinced of this figure. Though a few years ago Messrs Fortnum & Mason were marketing a teddy costing just the £125 each, made of mink. Now, who, might you ask, buys a mink Teddy? Older men, businessmen, according to Miss Snowdon, then the toy buyer at the shop.

'They buy them for their girlfriends,' reported Miss Snowdon to the *Evening News*, 'especially when they don't know the girl well enough to give her something more personal. It's a prestige gift. We're not exactly hoping to sell them by the dozen. We have sold two already.'

Personally I can't think of anything much more personal than an eighteen-inch Teddy Bear costing £125. This was in 1971 and I imagine it would be around the £200 mark now. But to be honest, they have abandoned selling them at Fortnums, or so a rather irritable lady reported to me on the blower the other day. I would have thought Arabs would be *mad* about them. A middle-aged gent queued all night at a slightly less prestigious store recently for a monster Teddy Bear. He *said* it was for his daughter but I'm not so sure. Nor apparently was the assistant, who eventually served him.

In America Teddy Bear buttons, in the form of cuff-links, can cost anything from 25 to 100 dollars a pair; a survival from Teddy Roosevelt's campaign days in the year of the bicentenary. The same year a well-known and rather dressy firm of tailors on Fifth Avenue were flogging Teddy Bear ties for children to give on Father's Day with the slogan 'Remember Your Teddy, Dad'.

Teddies are certainly working hard for their living as advertising symbols, and it is currently impossible to watch commercial television for a whole evening without catching a glimpse of one in an ad for cereals, electricity, stockings, and you name it.

The Electricity people feature a yellow bear in almost every promotion, which is what the National Coal Board did for so many years. Theirs was called Cosy and was every bit of fourteen inches high. He was usually shown carrying a full bucket of coal and his name was used to pin-point solid fuel warmings. The council actually had a live bear cub, called Cosy also, who took part in fuel exhibitions.

And then there is Chad, the dapper Teddy Bear with a top hat who is the trade mark of Bear Brand Ltd, the American hosiery manufacturers. He started life as a grizzly bear, which was thought too unattractive for promoting feminine merchandise. Talking of which I would like to remind you of the warm undergarment worn by ladies and approximating to old-fashioned combinations. It is of course called Teddy and up to recently Kayser-Roth were making them and, I hope, still are. At my prep school I was laughed at for wearing combies. But nowadays I suspect they would be considered rather kinky and chic, particularly if they were called Teddies.

Annual sales of Teddy Bears are estimated at around twenty million pounds. Despite the plethora of walkie-talkie dolls, spacemen, Action Men, rockets, killer-ray guns and now, thanks to *Jaws,* sharks, it is a fair bet that Teddy will occupy the honoured place on the pillow when bedtime comes. An international toy-making combine quizzed children to discover their favourite toy. It was a walk-over for Teddy.

But no one can pretend any longer that it is a child's prerogative to possess or desire a Teddy Bear of his own. It is proved over and over again that adults have a definite and equal need for the dear creatures. Only recently Mr Garth Nicholls, at that time Chairman of Lancaster University's Carmel College, asserted that the girl students there treasured them for their silent friendship and support. Almost every girl arrived with one and confirmed that they found Teddies cuddly, faithful and ideal subjects to whom they could confide their secrets.

It is curious how surprised people still are by the endless and seemingly inexplicable appeal of the Teddy Bear, as was demonstrated by the reaction to a triumphant exhibition a few years back in Brighton. What was meant to be a short Christmas season turned into a run of several months. Organized brilliantly and originally by Miss Marion Waller, the Curator of the National Toy Museum, it captured the imagination of everybody and both visits I paid to it showed its popularity. I went to the opening and gave a little talk to an audience ranging in age from four to eighty-four.

The display of bears was impressive indeed and not only the people of Sussex, but others from all over England, had lent their treasured friends. Many of them were arranged as Tableaux Vivants behind glass in front of an appropriate backcloth. There were bears on wheels, bears dressed as railway attendants, rakish bears and a wonderful Burlington Bertie. There were original manuscripts of Paddington and other famous literary bears, press cuttings, snaps and memorabilia of huge interest to the visitors.

I shan't easily forget my reception at the All Saints Infant School in Upper Norwood, London. When I arrived I was shown straight into the School Hall, where four hundred small people were sitting on the floor quiet as mice. The majority of them were clutching their Teddies. A teacher struck up 'The Teddy Bears' Picnic' on the piano and we were away on a most delightful afternoon. About thirty of the kids went up on the small stage and, one by one, without a visible trace of shyness, told a story about their own Teddy Bear. The theme was 'Why I love my Teddy'. At the end of this I told mine but curiously enough I was shy, perhaps because I had told it so often in a semi-professional way and it

44

14 Lambchop Fat Face, Pierre and Pohick

15 Gramps with Floppy, T-Bear and Hubert

16 Sitting in judgement

17 The Fitt bears at home

18 A captive audience for H.H's piano recital

19 *Right:* Olive Jones and Edward

20 *Below, left:* Mr Growler

21 *Below, right:* Burlington Bertie

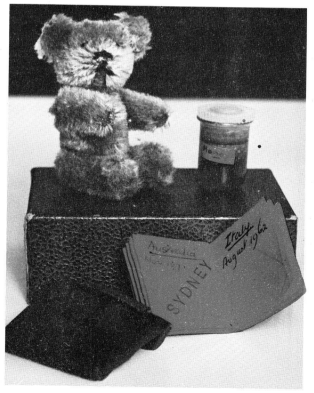

came out too pat. Later I was shown round an astonishing exhibition of drawings and paintings which the children had done and, when I left, I was presented with a tiny Teddy who had the school colours woven into him in the shape of a scarf.

The County of Kent is a great stronghold of arctophiles, enormously helped by Miss Jean Wright, who is in charge of the Children's Library at Ashford. In conjunction with the Kent County Council and the Kent Education Committee, she organized an exhibition under the title of 'A Hug of Bears' which was illustrated by a booklet of that title and listed every Bear book in print. This took place in 1972 and all of the books were on show. In addition to the literary output, the room was lined with an amazing number of bears lent by local people. The daddy of them all appeared to be a large sober-looking gentleman called Edward Hugh Trewartha. Charlotte Brown of Bybrook Junior School had brought her three bears and written a poem about each of them, and Candida Raymond contributed a selection from her hundred ditto.

For the enterprising visitor there was a display of bear-making equipment and instructions in the art of making Teddies, with some very handsome examples made locally. In 1976 a new edition of 'A Hug of Bears' was produced, which was even more comprehensive than the earlier one, and Miss Wright's efforts have obviously sparked off a whole spate of Teddy Bear functions.

A big feature of most of the goings-on mentioned above has been the competitive spirit. The difference in type between the senior and junior bears, displayed either in fact or fiction, has proved that in the main only their construction has radically altered. Instead of the kapok stuffing and gold mohair plush which distinguished the well-dressed bear of the pre-war days, we now seem to have nylon fur coats which can be washed. But even the most ghastly modern example can never be taken for anything but a Teddy Bear, though I fear my previous theory that no two ever look alike has been blown to smithereens by mass production.

I did once hear a story, never confirmed, that there was a special man employed by the firm of Steiff to see that no two similar animals ever left the factory, and that the same chap had to check that there was nothing remotely sinister in their faces. But, let's face it, everyone has their favourite friend and heaven help anyone who tries to prove that he (or in rare cases she) is exactly like *theirs*.

That is why Teddy Bear Competitions can be such fun, because of the different classes that can be held. Here I think is the moment to insert Colonel Henderson's excellent instructions on how to organize such an event. The good Colonel will, I am sure, forgive me if I just give extracts, but I know he would be delighted to send you a copy if you write to him at the address in the Appendix at the end of this book.

'The way to organize a Teddy Bear Competition in connection with a Bazaar,

Fete or Garden Party depends on what facilities can be provided in the way of suitable accommodation and helping workers. A church hall is ideal. Failing this, a really large marquee might do. As many volunteer workers as possible should be organized into groups as indicated below under the direction of a special committee.

'The bears are precious personal possessions, so they have to be well safeguarded from all risks all the time. They should be handed in on cloak-room tickets, for which pins or clips should be provided. Each bear must be labelled with the name and address of his owner and noted down on a list of entries, and at the end of the show must be given back only to the right owner with the correct ticket. The bears have to be guarded at all times (all night if need be).

'To ensure that a good number of bears are put on show at the outset and to encourage people to come early, free gifts (i.e. sweets or books etc) should be given to the first thirty (or so) bears entered for the competition.

'Three or four people will be required all day to attend to the labelling and ticketing of the bears. Four or five people must be ready to arrange the bears in groups on the shelves for display and judging and to mount guard over them in an area that must be roped off from public access.

'Some suitable Guest of Honour should be invited to present the prizes, and a well-qualified individual should be asked to act as Chief Judge, but at least two other judges should be appointed to help him. The best way to do the judging, which must go on continuously all day, is to have four or five tiers of shelves, roped off (or partitioned by string vertically) into different sections, one section for each prize group. At the top of each section its title should be displayed.

'As the bears come in they are put into the appropriate section on the lowest shelf. The judges then move the best in each section up to the second shelf. As the second shelf gets filled, the judges make a further selection and move some up to the third shelf, and so on. Likely prize-winners are finally put on the top shelf for the final judging.

'Easy access to all shelves in each section is essential. Shelves should be clean so as not to dirty the bears. To ensure *that bears do not fall over backwards,* they must be provided with boxes or other things to lean against.

'In any section where there are only a few bears, they should be arranged in groups looking at one another *as if having a picnic.* The floor in front must be kept clear for new arrivals. A good thing to do is to have a small flag on a pin for each section. This is put in the head of the leading bear' (Oh, Colonel Henderson, how *could* you?) 'and is moved into the best bear progressively as the show proceeds. At the time of final judging the prize-winners are thus all flagged, and can then be moved forward to a special table for the prize-giving. Each winning bear can be given a rosette to wear.' (That's better, Colonel H.)

'The public should be asked to assemble for the prize-giving at least five

49

minutes before the appointed time. The following groups are recommended for competition:

'1. Smallest; 2. Biggest (the first can be assembled in front of the second, who should be centrally placed); 3. Oldest; 4. Scruffiest (these types are interchangeable and should be placed beside each other); 5. Happiest; 6. Saddest (to judge the contrast best, these types should be placed beside each other); 7. Best Dressed; 8. Most original (one solution to a tie for the best-dressed bear); 9. Special prize for a Very Special Bear (generally presented by the Chief Judge). The requirements for this are that it must be cuddlesome, happy in expression, have fully jointed head, arms and legs, growl (all good bears growl), be suitable to be a life-long companion and easily transportable.

'To mobilize the Teddy Bears of a city, it has to be conducted like a military operation. At the end of the show the rush of people all clamouring to collect their bears must be controlled. They should be *lined up at each side and allowed to point out their bears three or four at a time,* passing out of the roped area at the other side and showing their labels and cloakroom tickets there for checking. *Nobody should be permitted to jump either the ropes or the queues.*

'*Statistics*

'Catering for 600 Bears between 2 and 4 pm means 5 persons labelling etc 1 per minute for 2 hours (5 x 120 = 600 Bears).

'Scaffolding (tubular) on shelves, in three tiers, 2 bears per foot for 600 bears = 300 foot of shelf or 3 layers of 100 ft (33 yds).'

So there you are. Couldn't be easier could it? Just pop out and book a church hall and/or a marquee and *get on with it.*

5 'A faithful fraternity of adults'

This is the phrase which the late lamented magazine *Life* used to describe a selection of people who had kept their Teddy Bears beside them all their lives. When my book appeared in the United States, the whole mystique of the subject amazed them so much that four pages in *Life* were devoted to it. I like to think that what *Life* treated as a sensational discovery came as very old hat to the examples they chose to feature in the article.

The heading they used was 'Teddy the Enduring Bear' with an underline 'aged and worn but faithful to the end'. In explanation the article pointed out that most children had a brief passionate attachment to a Teddy Bear and then moved on to other toys, but, to a faithful fraternity of adults the bear they had in childhood had become a lifelong companion. Such bears have survived fire and flood, the passage of years, the coming of children and grandchildren. Their owners used adjectives like 'placid', 'serene' and 'radiating contentment' to characterize their elderly friends.

Some of the people who contributed to the article are featured in my book anyhow, because I made my files available to the young lady who put the saga together but some of the others are more than worthy of a passing comment. For instance there is the Reverend Stephen Williamson of Wilkes-Barre, Pennsylvania. At the age of five, he found that not only were his parents going to have another child but they intended to call it Teddy. As he already had a Teddy, he informed them that it was out of the question because 'we can't have two Teddies in the same house'. So the incoming brother was called Robert and all was well in the household. 'Teddy still lives,' added the Reverend. 'We've been through too much together for me to throw him away. I often ask him how he is and tell him what kind of awful day I've had. He's old and distinguished and doesn't play any more.'

Then there's Shad (short for Shadrack) who belongs to Betty McDermid, who works in Public Relations for a New York firm. They have been together thirty-five years and Shad has spread his wings or paws no end since an article about him appeared in a Florida newspaper, when Betty was working there many years ago. He has pen pals all over the world. 'Shad spends his time,' said Miss McDermid, 'cheering and comforting people. In short he exists for one thing: to make life more bearable.' He has gathered a family round him which numbers more than a hundred. The Shad Pad is run on disciplined lines and, if the master is called away, Ignatz, a big blind bear once left on Miss McD's doorstep, steps in to assume command.

Water seems to offer a frequent hazard for bears and a number of them have fallen into lakes, rivers and seas. Seventy-year-old Teddy Rogers had a close call in Lake George when he and his owner fell overboard from a steamer. While drying out before the fire, he turned green, but survived, though he is sadly patched and has to wear clothes to hide his scars. However, he informed me in a letter that he can still *see* quite clearly, which is a Good Thing, as he is apparently boss of the house and Miss Emma Rogers trusts him with the housekeeping money.

The *Life* photograph is particularly moving as it shows him in smart football stockings, a wrist watch and a rather trendy hat, but the visible pieces of material on his limbs give some indication of the serious surgery he must have undergone.

'He knows me and loves me,' says Miss Rogers, a retired railroad law calendar clerk (a new profession to me but perhaps accounting for the wrist watch). 'I'll keep Teddy until God calls me, and after that they can do what they want with him.'

On the other hand, Rosemary Ritchie has very definite ideas about what is to happen to her friend, who is nearing seventy.

'I brought him from England and he always went to bed with me, even after I married, which didn't go over too well. He ended up in the corner. I've requested that Teddy be buried with me, for sentimental reasons. Who wants a Teddy Bear hanging around when the owner is no longer alive?'

I don't agree with Mrs Ritchie. Any bear on whom such obvious love and devotion has been poured should go out and Spread the Gospel or spend the remainder of his days in one of those lovely homes for Retired Bears, details of which you will find at the end of this book.

But there's no doubt that several people feel very strongly about what will happen to their friends after they die. Mrs Hadley, for instance, à propos of Sinnamon, has expressed the wish that 'he will hold up as long as I do. Then he will be cremated with me. These arrangements have all been made with the undertaker, who has seen him.'

52

Another lady, seventy years of age, has even inserted a codicil in her will. Her three-foot Teddy, whom she still treats with the utmost respect, will share her coffin.

The most off-beat of the couples in the *Life* feature appear to be Theodore Thau and his bear. He is an international trade expert for the department of commerce, and has had his bear since he was six months old and is rather caustic about him.

'He is less benign than most,' admits Mr Thau. 'Sometimes he frightens little girls. I don't know why. It's never bitten anyone as far as I know. In fact it has a very edible nose itself.' I must say, in the photo, Theodore Thau Teddy does look a tidge intimidating. Sitting bolt upright with an enormous nose, two very penetrating eyes and ears pushed well forward to enable their owner not to miss a trick, I doubt if he would stand for any sentimental nonsense.

So much for *Life* magazine, and now on to bears unsung and possibly only appreciated in the hearts of their owners and families. A lady of sixty who read my book was so stricken with guilt that she went straight to a suitcase and resurrected her first bear and her son's two. The former has an ear missing and some of his hair is worn off. 'But,' says Mrs Hertzman, 'he has a marvellously gentle expression and I swear his nose is always cold.'

The amount of trouble owners will take in order to keep their Teddies in trim is very heartwarming. A lady whose parents bought her a bear in July 1906 has never relaxed her devoted maintenance.

'His fur has worn smooth on the back of his head and about his face, but the rest of his body is still covered with the original soft, silky fur. He has his original rounded black button eyes, but I have reworked with black thread his nose, mouth and the claw marks on his hands and feet. Many years ago I restuffed his limp arms and legs and I have also made him many suits of clothes.

'No toy has ever been more loved and played with through the years. He has never been packed away in a box or left in storage. He has always been *in sight* somewhere in the house. At times he might have been put on a higher shelf or in a closet as protection from other children who might play too roughly with him, or from teasing brothers.

'My own three sons were born with the instinct not to mistreat him. As they grew older they each were given the Model of the Year. Many of these are still among their possessions.'

There is something very human about the name-dropping which goes on among the older generation when they talk about their Teddies. Mrs Wilkins lives in a Nursing Home in Tunbridge Wells but has never forgotten her visit with her Teddy to the States in 1907. They made great friends with Rudyard Kipling who was travelling in the same boat. The Teddy's name is Johnny and he's still the same (and I quote) 'beautiful Isabella brown colour'.

Another correspondent's bear came over *from* America and apparently spent a lot of the voyage sitting on Sir Winston Churchill's knee. Incidentally, Lady Wilson's bear is called Victor, and Theodore at this very moment is trying to find out the name of Mrs Enoch Powell's.

While on a political tack, American leaders seem pretty Teddy-orientated. Senator Teddy Kennedy still has the one given him by his father when he was eight years old and a bear sits proudly on the windowsill of the John F. Kennedy childhood home in Brookline, Massachusetts. In one room of the late President Johnson's ranch there is his crib and on it sits *his* Teddy. Teddies claim to have met their creator in person. No, I'm not being blasphemous. The most likely genuine candidate I have come across belonged to Mr Walter Pelham, who happened to be at Trinity College when President Theodore Roosevelt visited Cambridge University in 1905. Mr Pelham's daughter informed me that her father and another Trinity chap lowered the animal by means of a string to face Mr Roosevelt as he entered the quadrangle. One press report has it that the President actually stopped and shook hands with it. 'The bear hung on my father's study wall ever after,' wrote the lady, 'and was something to look at when being chastised, or lectured, or when asking for money or telling lies about where one had been.'

A great many adults don't get 'a thing' about Teddy Bears until they are, say, forty. I am thinking particularly of Mrs Batchelor, whom Oliver Q. Dodger owns (see Chapter 12). She doesn't remember having had a bear when she was a child. She did however have five children, and they all had Teddies and numerous other 'stuffed toys' that were well-loved and played with. But that's all they were. 'Stuffed toys.' In 1962 on a return trip from Germany Mrs Batchelor bought two black and white bears, Brigid and Erin, with her last two pounds. They were to take back to the two smallest children who had been left at home in Puerto Rico with their father.

'Brigid and Erin transformed our lives,' says Mrs Batchelor. 'They are rather old and battered now and their eyes are quite sunken in but they are the ruling heads of a bear colony which is growing by leaps and bounds.'

Mrs Graham of Halstead, Essex, wrote to me recently and, although she admitted to being seventy-eight years of age, she had never had a Teddy. She was confined to the house with arthritis and rheumatism and she said:

'I have always longed for one but never liked to buy one in case people laughed at me. Can you send me one, please, if you have him to spare?'

I could and did.

One thing my book helped to accomplish was to remove phobias and traumas about still caring for one's Teddy after a certain age.

'Your book did a great deal to help me dispel my sense of guilt, instilled by my otherwise tolerant mother, at keeping my own Teddy Bear who will be twenty this year,' so wrote a Surrey lady in 1973. 'Mercifully two years ago I met an amazing man who not only failed to laugh at Bear, but positively encouraged me to collect them. We are now married, and at the last count there were forty-five bears holding court in my armchair.'

A new twist was given by a lady who told me that her only solace during a very unstable childhood was a big Teddy Bear with orange-reddish hair. 'A series of unhappy marriages convinced me that I was unconsciously looking for my Teddy Bear and I eventually found a man who greatly resembles one. You see I took my original Teddy to my first marital home but he disappeared.'

One cannot help wondering how many shots the lady had had at matrimony before striking lucky. But you'd be *astonished* at how many ladies have confessed that they have married bear-like gents. I think it highly doubtful that it ever happens the other way round. I mean, I can imagine a man marrying a girl because she looked cuddly but not because she resembled a Teddy Bear. Though I did have a letter from a lady Bearess or so she described herself. She lived in Barcelona, of course. And in order to make this survey complete in every way, whatever the cost to the reader's feelings, here is the moment to tell you that three gentlemen, one a very big film star indeed, have admitted to having their first sexual experience with a Teddy Bear.

Some strong-minded ladies go as far as to announce publicly that 'Anyone who takes me must take my bears or stay out of my life'. I know one of these and her life seems completely bear-beset. Her Teddies' costumes vary from frilled gingham to lace-edged print and silk taffeta and some wear tiny bracelets and pendants round their necks. Their owner lives, or did some time ago, in a bed-sitting-room, and at night she 'borrows' her own bed from them and pops them into a large trunk which she bought for this very special purpose.

This habit of littering room(s) with Teddy Bears must disconcert sceptical callers quite often. Mine are out in the hall, ready to greet the visitor(s) and the latter can either say 'Ah, how sweet!' or shudder from top to toe and hurry into the comparatively bearless sitz-platz. A firm of chartered accountants called Tree & Son, of whom I wot, have seven bears, all of whom sit either on the settee or chairs. They are called Kerry Mac, Parker Hill, Kapeno, Upsi-Duck, What-a-Mythe, Edward Mode and Spook. You may well wonder where these exotic names come from. The bears are apparently called after horses or dogs on whom Tree & Son have won substantial sums. I can't think why they aren't Turf Accountants. Although the bears are kept mainly at home, one, I am assured, always takes pride of place at the boardroom table.

A couple in Washington have a small bear who is taken everywhere, put to bed at night and roused in the morning. He has jackets, sweaters and ties made for him. He has his own chair and his own banking account (accumulated from his weekly allowance and winnings on sporting events).

55

22 *Above, left:* Noele Gordon aged 2

23 *Above, right:* Helen Walton's first bear

24 *Left:* Hazel Pollock and friend

25 Restored bear (courtesy of Mrs Sanderson)

26 Ted Moore, comforter

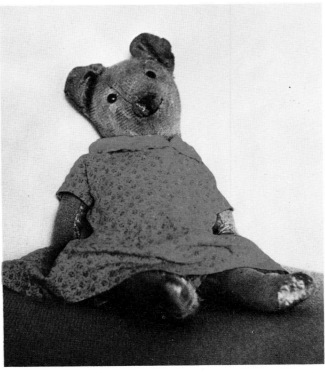

27 Miss Theodora Fenton

28 A Chicago welcome from the Cody bears

TEDDY ON THE BEACH.

'Neither my husband or I would be surprised to come home in the evening and see him walking about our apartment,' states the wife. 'It all began about nine years ago when occasionally I would scold my husband for his shortcomings. Then we saw a picture in a newspaper of a small polar bear being spanked by his mother for bad behaviour. The little bear was sitting down, his back to a wall, with his front paws over his eyes, crying. After which, whenever I scolded my dear husband, he would assume this pose. At Christmas that year I gave a bear to my husband, little knowing the position he was to assume. And that is of a Spoiled Child. He must have his way or say. We leave lights and the TV on for him in the evening. Oddly enough, some of our friends think we are a little peculiar.'

I wonder what their friends would have thought of the Dalys of Essex. 'Our chaps rather like to feel they are among the best-dressed bears in the country. They have at least two summer and two winter suits each plus caps and boots, and our Number 3 bear, who is rather naval, has been heard to talk about going into "blues" or "whites".' The wardrobe is supplied by Mrs Daly's mother.

The wife of a Scots judge has a collection of thirteen bears, all dressed in naval uniform, from ratings to one full admiral. My young informant, a relative of the lady, was fairly surprised to see them ranged in line on her drawing-room sofa, and flabbergasted a few days later when she went to see her off on a long journey by train. 'For there, in the railway carriage, were all the bears taking up a whole side. I cannot remember anyone offering any comment, so I suppose I took it as one of the inexplicable things which grown-ups did.'

It isn't reported whether the little extra passengers were charged their fare. I do know a case of a lady on a London bus who had to pay for her two large Teddies who were accompanying her. Their tummies were rumbling so much (they must have been 'Growlers', who were all the rage at the time) that an insensitive conductor made her pay (half price).

The wife of a big American executive, Carolyn Wechsler, likes bears. She's got them propped up on couches, sprawling on floors, hanging on walls, lined up on shelves, anchored in glass cases, arranged on her dresser and on her person (a gold and diamond brooch).

'When I was a very little girl,' said Ms Wechsler, 'I found a teddy bear's head buried in the sand on the beach. My brother and I searched for hours to find that little bear's body. We finally found it and sewed the bear back together. He was my first bear and I had him until he couldn't be repaired any more.

'When Norman and I got married twenty-eight years ago we moved to Detroit. My brother shipped my very favourite bear of all (Theodore) to our new place. When Norman, my husband, walked in one night Theodore' (who is three feet tall, brown and has been affiliated with Ms Wechsler for forty-six years) 'was sitting in the hall.

'I said, "Now, look, Norman, *we've* been married for forty-eight hours. And you might as well get used to it right now. Where I go, Theodore goes." '

In the following years of their marriage, Theodore has lived in seven cities, has been dressed up for his birthday and other social occasions, has had tea parties, cocktail do's and dinners given in his honour and has received postcards, letters and telegrams.

For all his fast living, in his photo he looks pretty solid.

'Oh yes!' Ms Wechsler agreed. 'Doesn't he look just terrific? Well it's not by accident. He's been redone three times at the taxidermist's.'

She told me about another ardent arctophile, the late Frank Crowninshield who used to edit *Vanity Fair* magazine.

'He had a gorgeous bear who had his own dinner jacket and tails and ties and the works. Frank would take his bear to dinner with him, and do you know that every course that was served to Frank was served to his bear too.'

I am indebted to Miss Marian McEvoy of *Woman's Wear Daily* for all the Wechsler information.

Do you know what happens when a Bear-Orientated couple spilt up? A typical case is that of the Middleditches.

Henry Middleditch, an Insurance Broker, sued his former wife for the return of an eighteenth-century table, a cut-glass decanter and his Teddy Bear.

The lady who picked out this item commented very perceptively on it in a local paper: 'Mr Middleditch has my complete sympathy and I hope an understanding judge gave him immediate custody of a bear which probably didn't mean so much to his wife. The only thing that bothers me is why did he leave it behind in the first place? When I finally put away childish things in favour of a husband and family, I brought my Teddy Bear with me, and until just a few years ago he lay in our attic, comfortably wrapped in tissue paper in a shoe box marked Please Burn, so that my heirs and assignees would dispose of him decently. After all he has been my friend and security blanket through most of the years of my growing up and faded, shabby and threadbare, he was still dear. Eventually, for reasons I cannot fathom, I followed my own directions and cremated him myself,with a secret sentimental tear for all he represented.' So wrote Mrs James Dow McCallum.

Teddies are no strangers to the law courts, as was hinted at in the first chapter. I even know one (though not intimately) who was produced as evidence of adultery. Not as a co-respondent, I hasten to add. And a few years back in a trial at the Old Bailey, a small blue nylon Teddy sat with a card round his neck, labelled 'Exhibit no 56'. He was partly responsible for jailing two men for receiving stolen cars and, after the trial, he was brought back to Amanda, his owner, by the Detective Sergeant in charge of the case.

People keep on stealing bears as well as cars and three hundred of them disappeared from a warehouse in Shoreditch. They were two feet high, had noses of black plastic and bells on their ears, which I'm afraid they didn't ring loudly enough as they were not recovered.

There was also the bizarre occurrence outside Rochdale, when a lorry driver on his way to Leeds from a Teddy Bear factory, didn't realize that scores of the little dears (well, fairly big dears in this case) had slipped off his vehicle. It was one o'clock in the morning and a home-going motorist found himself in Teddy Bear Land.

People were hurrying along the road clutching armfuls of Teddies. Other motorists drove past with bears peering out of every window. He began to feel out of place without a Teddy Bear of his own. And when he got home, he decided to telephone the police and find out if they knew anything about an outbreak of Teddy Bears.

To his surprise, they said they did, because the lorry driver had just phoned to say that one hundred and fifty bears, some pink and white, some brown and white, had disappeared into the night. One witness had reported that he had seen a motorist stuff forty of them into his car.

Inspector Cape, chief of Rochdale Police Division, said, 'We want those Teddy Bears back. They may be very cuddly and tempting to take home. But they are worth £3 each and there can be no question of a Teddy Bear amnesty.'

On another occasion a Police Constable was cleared of stealing a bear. His defending counsel advanced the plea, a little incongruously I think, 'Is a man of his age, getting towards the end of his service in the force, likely to take a Teddy Bear, intending to *keep* it?'

I'm here to tell you that Teddy Bears, particularly Senior Citizens fetch fantastic prices these days and anything up to £200 is quite usual. Shirley Temple's big brown Teddy that appeared in the film *Captain January* fetched over that sum at an auction at Twentieth- Century Fox Studios a few years ago. I wonder if he was the same one who starred with her and Gary Cooper in *Wee Willie Winkie?*

As is only to be expected in an industry which relies so heavily on luck, mascots, and totems, all branches of the entertainment business have arctophiles all over the place.

Miss Noele Gordon, probably the most popular television personality in Britain, says she takes her Teddy very seriously and that she's met human beings who didn't have half the personality he has.

On the other hand Jill Bennett (Mrs John Osborne) has a sort of love-hate relationship with Sir Teggy. 'I've had Sir Teggy longer than I've been alive. My mother bought him in Penang two weeks before I was born. Sir Teggy is bolshie, vile, unpleasant, fascist and I hate him but if I don't take him along everywhere he'll never forgive me. He's got earrings now and gone all poofy.' I would be

64

seriously worried about Sir Teggy's future if the reporter hadn't added, 'She laid down Sir Teggy fondly.'

Lynn Redgrave always takes her bear to the theatre and he used to keep Theodore company when we were appearing together in *Black Comedy* in New York. I expect they talked about their operations most of the time because Lynn's had three (on Bexhill Beach) for squeak removal.

Jean Marsh, the lovely 'Upstairs, Downstairs' lady, was a great comfort on a TV show we both did in America as she admitted to being lost over there without her twenty-two-year-old bear.

Dame Margot Fonteyn and her husband were greatly comforted, I believe, by a Teddy during his illness, and Nadia Nerina is another dancer who is bear-minded.

Paul Scofield at one time was so bear-minded that, as a child, he stole one. I hasten to add that he was persuaded to give it back.

Richard Hearne, the immensely philanthropic comedian, has a disreputable bear of nearly sixty, which he found in a basement. His wife says, 'The bear is patched and darned but it's jealously guarded. I tried to throw it away once or twice and got into the most frightful trouble.' And rightly!

Elvis Presley was tremendously keen on the whole mystique until he sang the number 'Teddy Bear' which brought him roughly one thousand, nine hundred and twenty-six of the species from fans.

And for the younger generation, you will almost certainly know that when Stuart Wood, of the Bay City Rollers, collapsed exhausted on stage in Melbourne, Australia, he went to bed cuddling his Teddy Bear.

'Five minutes later Woody bounced back and completed the show.'

Well, that's what the report said verbatim. So you do see . . . in the world of the Teddy Bear, miracles still happen.

6 Bear Hall of fame

It's about time we stopped considering people and their attitudes to Teddies and started on the Bear Roll of Honour. We have many famous and distinguished bears of whom to be proud and I think it is only right and proper to lead off with the One Who Climbed the Matterhorn. My authority is no less substantial than the curator of the Alpine Museum, Zermatt, Mr Karl Lehner, who sent me the information in French.

It appears that an Italian Alpine Climber called Walter Bonnati conquered the north slopes of the mountain on February 22 1965. It took him the best part of five days and he doubts if he could have done it without the help of a Teddy he carried in his rucksack, who belonged to the children of the local hotel Alpenblick. He was small, yellow and very adventurous.

The first three nights were just bearable but on the fourth Mr Bonnati was in despair. There was a terrible wind and the cold was lethal. His morale was at zero and it was impossible to sleep, because snow was falling from the sky, freezing on him as it did so. It was such agony that the thought of cutting the rope and ending it all in a few seconds seriously entered his mind.

Suddenly he remembered the Teddy Bear and took him out of his comparatively warm hiding place. He spent the night talking to him on a wide variety of subjects and even got as far as confessing his 'sins' (I cannot think of an alternative translation for 'péché') and the Teddy listened with rapt attention. When the first light of dawn came, he was still listening to the climber's unfinished life story.

Mr Bonnati pressed on to the top of the mountain and, on his return, told the owners that their little friend had saved his life. So, if any of you are thinking of

66

attempting the Matterhorn, I would advise you to get in touch with the Pannatier children, because their Teddy Bear Zissi will direct you straight to the summit.

A British bear to be proud of is Mr Woppit, who belonged to the late Donald Campbell. He was without doubt the fastest Teddy in the world. The two first met in 1957 when Peter Barker, who was Campbell's manager, placed the animal in the cockpit of the jet-propelled Hydroplane *Bluebird* before Donald made his attempt on the world's water speed record. Mr Woppit has three records to his credit, as a matter of fact, for he achieved 260.3 miles an hour at Coniston Water in May 1959. He was also with Donald when they both survived the fastest automobile crash in history on the Bonneville Salt Flats in Utah in 1960. They were travelling in the Proteus *Bluebird* and Donald described the horror he felt afterwards lying in hospital with a fractured skull, when he realized that Mr Woppit was still in the cockpit. An urgent radio message was dispatched and the bear was given a police escort to the hospital. On being X-rayed it was discovered that Mr Woppit had his nose a bit out of joint, but was otherwise none the worse for his adventure.

He is described as being of slightly foxy appearance, eight inches high and a cross between a koala and a baby bear. He is made of light brown fur fabric and wears green shoes and a rather tight scarlet jacket. His ears are green-lined too! He is named after a character which appeared in the first number of a popular children's comic called *Robin.*

Mr Woppit has now travelled at 403 mph on land. To have been the fastest on land *and* sea has so far only been achieved by Sir Malcolm and Donald Campbell and Mr Woppit, and the latter is unfortunately the sole survivor. He was found floating face downward after the tragedy which killed his friend Donald at Coniston Water on 4 January 1967. He is now cherished by Donald Campbell's widow, Tonia Bern, the cabaret star.

Another Teddy cast in the heroic mould, who has perhaps had greatness thrust upon him, is Rupert who belongs to Janet, the daughter of George Villiers, the BBC cookery expert. The family were escaping from Nazi-occupied Norway during World War II, and the only possession they had been able to salvage in their haste was Rupert. They found themselves adrift in the North Sea and making for the Shetland Islands when a British Reconnaissance plane flew low over them. Janet was instructed to make Rupert wave at it. This she did and later they were told that it was he who convinced the plane's crew that the refugees must be British. I can only hope that Rupert was not a Steiff bear because, if he was, he must have felt a bit of a traitor.

There are numerous cases of refugee bears. When the Flanderer family were expelled from Carlsbad in Bohemia just after the war, they were only allowed to take very few personal belongings, but teddy had to be one of them. Elisabeth

Flanderer says she would gladly have left everything else behind. So he came to Western Germany and has settled down happily in Munich.

Mrs Batchelor, who is owned by Oliver Q. Dodger, has several defectors from behind the Iron Curtain. She refuses to be specific in case it endangers the future of their relatives or friends who, it is understood, can't wait to defect themselves.

An exceptionally astute bear from behind the IC is Edward Bear, who was born there. At an early age (judging by state and colour of fur, lines on paws, etc) he made up his mind to leave. He crossed into Switzerland and got himself hidden in a bedside cupboard in a clinic frequented by foreigners.

There Mr Carr, a high-ranking British civil servant, found him and felt empowered to offer him political asylum. Mrs Carr was delighted to welcome the defector into her houshold and hastily knitted him a jacket. Her husband lent him an old tie, which he has never returned as a matter of fact. He has been everywhere with the Carrs and crossed the Atlantic in the SS *United States*.

Teddies have never flinched from danger and it was no surprise to me to hear that one called 'Spud' was a member of a Scottish Parachute Regiment and had made many successful jumps. He is, it must be confessed, attached to the Yorkhill Hospital in Glasgow, which could be handy.

But pride of place in this sort of endeavour must surely go to SUO Edward Bear of the Royal Military Academy at Sandhurst. He has made over three hundred descents and has a uniform similar to that of an officer cadet. He also possesses his own parachute and has been frequently decorated.

To go to the opposite extreme I have had a communication from a Teddy who claims to have been the first to ascend to the Space Deck of the World's Tallest Free-Standing Structure. Or that's what he *says*. Anyhow it's in Toronto and his companion has sent in a report:

'A friend and I decided to visit the CN Tower two days after it opened and Teddy bravely announced his intention of accompanying us. The other bears were all very excited and helped him give his fur a specially good brushing so he would look his best. We were all afraid of accidents in the crowds if I carried him in my arms, so the bears put their heads together and came up with a safe mode of transport.

'Teddy travelled downtown in an airline shoulder-bag. At the foot of the Tower he stood up inside it with his elbows resting comfortably on the rim, my arm around his middle like a seat belt. This made us both feel secure and left his view unobstructed as we rode up in the glass-walled elevator ("My ears don't even block up," observed Teddy) and walked round the observation decks looking at the breath-taking vistas.

"I am the First Teddy Bear in the World to see all this," said Teddy ecstatically. The World's Highest Post Office was not yet open for business nor was the World's Highest Restaurant, so he could not avail himself of their facilities.

'Back on the ground, Teddy declared himself exhausted from standing so long and his heart was beating rather fast with the excitement of it all, so he curled up in his airline-bag for a zizz while we had lunch and travelled home. The other bears were agog to hear his account of the Great Ascent and they all expect to dine out on it in Toronto Bear Society for at least a year.'

Of course it is no news to any of us arctophiles that bears are extremely adventurous and daring. It did surprise me, however, to learn that two Teddies should literally go to Timbuctu within a few months of each other. Timbuctu is usually a place you jokingly send people to, but in this case these intrepid bears went there more or less of their own accord. Timbuctu in the Republic of Mali (née French Sudan) is also the place where Major Gordon Laing, an explorer, was murdered.

Mrs Ruth de la Mare and her husband, then of Stroud, Glos, travelled in a Land Rover from Tangier to Timbuctu in November 1972. Ruth took her Teddy, named Major Laing after the famous murderee. They followed a very circuitous and dodgy route and finished up by going through the Niger River Valley. The local negro children were apparently bewildered by the bear. They had never seen anything remotely like it apparently, which I don't find hard to believe.

The next year Patrick and Mollie Matthews, who do the delightful books, TV films and postcards of Teddy Edward, decided to take *him* to Timbuctu. I would like to be able to report that the natives said, 'Oh, lawks! Not another Teddy Bear. The place is getting overrun with them,' but the Matthewses say that the Tuaregs, Dogons, Bozos and Peuhls (I just *love* typing that sort of thing!) were most friendly to Teddy Edward. There has been a certain amount of T. Bear rivalry about who *was* the first to reach Timbuctu but certainly, to keep the peace, there is no doubt that Teddy Edward was the first to make it by boat. Anyhow his adventures on this particular expedition and indeed all over the world can be heard, seen and read everywhere.

Another much-travelled bear is called Edward and has a passport complete with picture and paw-mark. He also carries a smart brown suede dispatch case (3.3 cm by 2.8 cm) bearing the initials E.B. to put the passport in with a small pot of honey. He has made friends all over the world, visited the first Flying Saucer House, met the Mayoress of Escondido and has just got back from New Zealand. Next stop Russia.

His owner is a Miss Olive Jones, a retired schoolteacher who numbers two other notable bears in her collection. One is made of golden-coloured tin and has been a member of the household for sixty-five years. He is almost flat with surface markings and rattles when shaken as though he contains grains of rice. Another favourite of hers is the Chief, of about the same vintage. He has black boot-button eyes and a growl. There was a purse in his back and this was modernized over thirty years ago by the addition of a zip-fastener. At the same time he was fitted with a new growl but when he returned from hospital, he would only growl when turned upside down.

Many bears, and their friends, have written in to say that they are the Oldest Teddy Bear in the World and as yet I have been unable to get near proving any of their claims. Apart from the original Presidential one (which I will discuss later), Colonel Henderson may very easily have the winner in his family.

A delightful letter was sent to the Worthing Museum, accompanying a venerable Teddy for their collection, from a Mrs Taunt. 'On the evening of December 15 1903 I was expected to be born. Dr Cope of Westminster was summoned. He in turn called his coachman who was so keen for me to be born that he made a mad dash across London to fetch Nurse Clutterbuck. I duly arrived before midnight on the 15th and the Doctor and his coachman were so delighted that the next day they presented me with a Teddy Bear. This I still have, a little battered perhaps and without its groaning voice after many baths, but still fit enough to be included in your exhibition.'

Another hot contender for the title of OBITW is Sir Edward Bear Bt, who belongs to young Elizabeth Rimer of Ilford. He was bought in Switzerland by her great-grandfather and has had a bit of renovating since 1904, several new noses and a smart set of brown suede paws. He has also lost his voice but his eyes are still his own and he has his hump. Manufacturers stopped putting humps on Teddies around 1908 and if you run across a behumped bear you may be sure that he's nearly seventy, so pay him a great deal of respect.

Around that period there were many bears on wheels. Some had cords attached to their shoulders, which made them growl when they were pulled and why not, for heaven's sake? Wouldn't you under similar circumstances? The 'Growlers' were much in demand, and I heard an amusing story of one who was sent through the post. The parcel was delivered by a policeman who had instructions to watch it opened because the sender was suspected of contravening the law by sending a live animal through the post. Ah happy days! Nowadays no one would dare touch it, would they, except the Bomb Disposal Unit? Anyhow the happy recipient still remembers the blood-curdling growls which emerged every time the parcel was tilted.

A close friend of Theodore's called Edward Bear, who lives in Wells, Somerset, had a certain amount of trouble with his growl when he was young. He is now close on sixty but has an astonishing memory for detail. He joined the family (called Berman. Edward can't imagine what happened to the other 'a') soon after the end of the '14–'18 War as a companion to a little girl of two.

'When the little girl was four or five,' wrote Edward Bear, 'she decided to make me growl fortissimo: she jumped on my growler chords which suffered irreparable damage and it was only about fifteen years ago that medical science

70

supplied me with a grafted growl (of higher pitch but I accepted it). Soon after the loss of my growl, too active participation at a party caused my head to come off, and while awaiting transport to the hospital, I had the most undignified experience of my life. The girl's parents, their bridge guests and two maids of the household played a round game called "Broken Bottles" with my head in the hall late at night. Never have I suffered such lack of respect.'

I am happy to report that after the little girl grew up, Edward Bear acquired the dignity and respect to which he was entitled. In fact, he became a sort of Elder Statesman and, truth to tell, a tidge overbearing: 'My influence is paramount in the family now; sometimes only I can persuade the boys during their vacations that it is high time to get up. Politically we are all very Right Wing. Certainly we are charitable and have no wish to Grind the Faces of the Poor but I know where to draw the line and I expect it to be toed... Be so kind as to let me know if I can be of any further assistance to you. I shall be indeed interested in the ultimate results of your researches.

'With sentiments distingués from us all.

I am yours very truly,

Edward Bear.'

But when he came to Theodore's party at Brown's Hotel to launch the book, he turned out not to be stuffy at all. In fact he was one of the Lives and Souls of it.

Have you noticed how many bears are called Edward? In a British survey concerning three hundred and fifty bear-owning children, it was disclosed that forty-five per cent of them called their friend Teddy because, as so many rightly pointed out, 'He is a Teddy'. Many of them had actually added in the questionnaire *of course*, as though Teddy was the only available name, but most adults favour Edward. Five per cent of the children favoured dimunutives of the word and Tedkin, Big Ted, Little Ted or plain Ted were much in evidence. One lady bear rejoiced in the name of Tedwina because, as was carefully explained, 'he's a she and not a him'.

Popular choices among the remainder were Pooh (of course), Panda, Brumas, Candy, Honey, Syrup and Toffee. Descriptive names such as Cuddles, Tubby, Growly, Wooly, Ginger or Curly were quite common, and of the really unusual names, practically all of them had been bestowed by an imaginative father. These included Polyphemus ('because he has only one eye'), Pythagoras ('because my sister hates geography'), Gladly ('this last because he's cross-eyed and there's that hymn which starts "Gladly my cross I'd bear" '). I did meet a lady the other day who had called her bear Disgusting which amused me greatly, particularly as she seemed devoted to him. It's odd that Theodore is so seldom used, although I never wavered at my bear's christening.

Two very popular, comparatively new names are Sooty and Paddington. The original of the former is a real bear, as you probably know, and a chance meeting

39 600 feet up!

between him and Harry Corbett led to Fame and Fortune for both parties. It all started in April 1949 when Harry was strolling along the North Pier at Blackpool.

'It's funny,' he remarked in his rich Bradford accent to the *Sunday Express*, 'but when really important things happen in your life you never realize it at the time or guess where your steps are leading you. I only know that on this particular day I stopped to look in the window of this toy-shop. I was just turning to walk away when he caught my eye. This glove puppet — a little yellow bear. Even now I can't tell you exactly what it was about him. But I just couldn't leave him. He looked so appealing.'

So the 7/6d tag (37½p to you youngsters) was removed and the little bear that was to transform Harry Corbett's life left the toy-shop in a brown paper parcel.

'I was entertaining at children's parties in the evenings to bring in a little extra money,' said Harry, 'and I started using the little bear (I called him Teddy then) to help me do magic tricks.'

Three years later Harry Corbett and Teddy appeared in a closed circuit television talent show. Their impact was so great that they were asked to appear *live* on a children's TV programme and after that they made show-biz history. From being an engineer surveyor Harry was offered six programmes by the BBC for which he was to be paid twelve guineas each. The snag was that they were fortnightly, so it seemed a dotty exchange for his secure and basic salary of £15 a week in his old job, plus a car and perks.

He talked it over with his wife Marjorie, and decided to take the plunge. He threw up his job, changed Teddy's appearance, gave him black ears and called him Sooty. For fifteen years the bear reigned supreme at the BBC children's programmes and then, suddenly in 1968, the Corporation decided to axe the pair. Howls of protest went up and tots started writing threatening letters. But it all ended happily when Sooty was put on the market and was snapped up by Thames Television with a £30,000 contract. He is now the highest-earning puppet in the world and can usually be seen *live* in a London theatre around Christmas-time.

But, alas, Harry Corbett recently had a heart attack and turned over the entire Sooty empire, including girl-friend Soo and the long-eared dog, Sweep, to his son, Matthew.

Matthew, who is not yet thirty, describes Sooty's appeal: 'It's his naughtiness, really. He does all the things children would like to do themselves, such as throwing a custard pie at their father. It helps them to get rid of pent-up emotions.' But Harry has not left his old friend entirely — he stays on as 'consultant'.

Another bear entertainer climbing rapidly up the ladder of fame is Nookie, who assists the ventriloquist Roger de Courcey or vice versa. The pair have

74

appeared at the Palladium, and in the last Royal Command Performance. Roger says he has never looked back since he bought his first Teddy Bear at a jumble sale. The only trouble is that he has already worn out five Nookies since the act started and no one has dared to ask him where they have gone.

Finally we come to probably the most distinguished living bear, and before you all jump down my throat, remember that Winnie the Pooh, to whose history and career I am going to devote a whole chapter, is not *owned* by any single person. The one I'm thinking of is Archibald Ormsby-Gore, the property of our Poet Laureate, Sir John Betjeman, CBE. I think some decoration should be dished out to Mr Ormsby-Gore for the pleasure he has given the world and his owner in the flesh, so to speak, and in the written word.

'Archie has been with me as long as I can remember,' says Sir John, 'he is about a foot high when he is sitting down and is very patched. His eyes are wool, his ears and nose are of some kind of cloth. Originally he was of golden fur. This only survives on his back and behind. He is very Protestant-looking:

> 'Safe were those evenings of the pre-war world
> When firelight shone on green linoleum;
> I heard the church bells hollowing out the sky,
> Deep beyond deep, like never-ending stars,
> And turned to Archibald, my safe old bear,
> Whose woollen eyes looked sad or glad at me,
> Whose ample forehead I could wet with tears,
> Whose half-moon ears received my confidence,
> Who made me laugh, who never let me down.
> I used to wait for hours to see him move,
> Convinced that he could breathe. One dreadful day
> They hid him from me as a punishment:
> Sometimes the desolation of that loss
> Comes back to me and I must go upstairs
> To see him in sawdust, so to speak,
> Safe and returned to his idolater.'

The above is an excerpt from *Summoned By Bells*, an autobiography in verse by Betjeman, in which he pays tribute to his companion of nearly sixty-five years' standing, to say nothing of sitting.

'Who made me laugh, who never let me down' seems to me to sum up two of Teddy's main virtues pretty succinctly, and 'Convinced that he could breathe' explains the secret belief of so many children.

Later in the book, the poet, quoting the words of 'Maud, my hateful nurse' describes her reaction to this being late:

  ' "You're late for dinner, John", I feel again
That awful feeling, fear confused with thrill,
As I would be unbuttoned, bent across
Her starchy apron, screaming, "Don't, Maud! Don't!"
Till dissolution, bed and kindly fur
Of aged, uncomplaining Archibald.'

Some years ago I was privileged to meet Mr Ormsby-Gore, when he kindly invited Theodore and H.H. to bring me to lunch. We had a rather spectacular journey because in those days Sir John resided in the delightfully named Cloth Fair, which is situated in the depths of the City just behind Smithfield Market. As I rounded the latter, a group of burly butchers, clearly TV addicts, bawled out, 'Got your Teddy with you, Mister?' 'Certainly,' I replied, producing my little lot from my pocket. The butchers swore horribly but good-humouredly.

'Please desist,' I admonished them. 'Theodore *hates* bad language.'

Later I discovered that Mr Ormsby-Gore felt rather the same. In fact, he is even stricter about codes of behaviour than most of his fellows. We have had several letters from him on this very subject; here is an extract from one:

'On behalf of my Fellow Bears I wish to thank you for the mention you made of us, I understand, on the Television. Nevertheless, I feel it incumbent on me to point out that no True Believer in the Triune Covenant-Keeping Jehovah can approve of a medium which indiscriminately talks to the Saved and the Damned. I hope I shall have the pleasure of meeting some of your bears soon and leading them through Sovereign Grace out of Eternal Torment into Light.

  'Yours faithfully'

After I first met Mr Ormsby-Gore, I formed the impression that he was a Baptist who strongly disapproved of drinking and smoking, and led a pretty exemplary life. Sir John regards him as a sort of conscience but they get on well enough. I didn't, I hope tactfully, bring up the provocative subject of religion but I asked Theodore to write to Archibald for clarification.

Mr Ormsby-Gore replied in characteristic fashion:

'Dear Theodore,
'I spend much of my time thinking of the futility of mankind and the Last Judgement, when all but us Strict and Particular Baptists will be consigned to everlasting flames. I can find scriptural warrant for all of this. I therefore give your friend, Mr Peter Bull, permission to make use of the quotation he mentions, as in eternity, which I constantly contemplate, it is of no importance.

  'Yours in the sure and certain hope etc'

This particular letter had a P.S. 'A secretary is typing this, as my paws are too thick for my American-built machine.'

Archibald, as you can see, has a strong personality, which is not surprising, as he has been greatly influenced by his friend, who is one of the most loved, revered and influential people in Great Britain. Sir John's efforts to conserve buildings of traditional heritage, beauty and interest and his constant warring against the sheer ugliness and noisy nastiness of so-called progress have endeared him to thousands. He has genuine warmth and a real care for humanity.

Recently during his seventieth birthday celebrations there was a TV programme in which he did allow a photo of himself when a child holding his friend, but he drew the line at having himself doing ditto in 1976 on the front cover of the *Radio Times*. So at the last moment a copy of *Tiger Tim's Weekly* was substituted.

'Whose woollen eyes looked sad or glad at me.' That's it, isn't it, really?

7 Lost property dept (bears)

I thought you'd like to know that out of every four hundred thousand articles lost on London Transport every year, about three hundred are Teddy Bears. In almost every case they are claimed immediately.

For a dyed-in-the-fur arctophile like myself it is inconceivable to think of anyone *losing* a bear but it does seem to happen quite often. And not everyone can be as lucky as the small Londoner who was travelling to the country with his Nanny, brother and Teddy. At the station he would lean out of the window and dangle the bear by the legs, and, as the train drew away from the platform, the inevitable happened. Teddy fell. Small boy, Nanny and brother all screamed at the only porter within screaming distance: 'We live at No. 1, Cheyne Gardens, Chelsea.'

The train sped away, the little chap was distraught during the whole of his stay in the country, but imagine his delight when he arrived home to find Teddy waiting for him, neatly parcelled by the porter. The next day he took his bear and his Nanny off to Liverpool Street Station to deliver thanks in person.

A family of five go to the church of Santa Maria Sopra Minerva every time they are in Rome, to give thanks at St Anthony's altar for the recovery of a Teddy Bear they lost some years ago, which turned up in that church.

A small boy, who couldn't swim, jumped into the River Severn to save his (bear) friend from drowning. The boatman, who saved the boy, realized the value of the greying moth-eaten bear and rowed upstream to rescue him too.

And American kids are just as brave. My partner, Mr Busby, saw his Teddy being swept away by flood waters which were swirling round the family residence in Northport, Washington State. As he couldn't swim it was just as well his father was around, or it might be me having to work out the VAT at Zodiac the Astrological Emporium. (Advt, as usual.)

Another small boy, called Graham White, fought a fire for twenty minutes to save two Teddy Bears. He didn't have time to dial 999. There was also a boy knocked down by a van, who said 'Teddy's hurt too' when the ambulance arrived.

An extraordinary saga of a lost bear started in Sydney, Australia, when Diane, an Air New Zealand purser, found him in an empty plane. He was all alone and looked quite forlorn, having no doubt been greatly loved by some child, now broken-hearted at his loss.

Diane checked everywhere. Air crews were enlisted in the search for his owner, but nobody laid claim to him. Consequently a world-wide enquiry was started, in which personnel of a dozen airlines tried to find Teddy's owner.

A globe-circling odyssey of the little lost bear started. On June 21 1975 Diane got an Air New Zealand crew to fly the bear to Christchurch and later Auckland. Finding no trace of the owner at either place, the crews passed the bear on to other airlines with wide-ranging destinations.

In this way Teddy became quite a celebrity. He was given a log book in which his travels were recorded. Before long he became adorned with flight wings, air labels and sundry other tags. Word of the high-flying bear spread among air crews all round the globe and his log book was filled with entries and departures from such exotic places as Hong Kong, Tahiti, Bermuda, New York, Jamaica, Johannesburg, Rio de Janeiro, and Heathrow.

Though Customs inspectors in the various countries co-operated with the air crews and stamped Teddy's log book with appropriate markings, he was adjudged a 'non-person' and was not allowed entry into any of the countries at which he touched down. This is why that Teddy's true story has a fairytale ending.

The adventures of the little bear so captivated the imagination of his American sympathizers that on July 22 1975 they entered in his log a record of Teddy having an audience with Queen Elizabeth at Buckingham Palace. Her Majesty, taking into account his global achievements (he had by then flown one hundred and fifty thousand miles and had been up in the sky for more than three hundred hours) dubbed him Sir Edward Roosevelt Bear.

The newly-created knight was reunited with his owner on September 7 at Los Angeles International Airport. What had happened was this. Jamie Fowler, aged four, was asleep when he and his mother left the Teddy Bear behind in the plane at Singapore, and in the bustle of changing planes, Mrs Fowler failed to report his loss. To comfort young Jamie when he woke up he was given a Koala Bear, but even at that age, you know what's what in the Teddy Bear World, and he hankered after his old friend.

So Mrs Fowler wrote home to New Zealand and told her husband what had

79

happened. The Air New Zealand agents were alerted, wheels were put in motion and Jamie was able to greet Teddy, when he and his mother boarded a flight home to Wellington, New Zealand.

Another story with a happy ending is that of a Teddy Bear left in a car that was stolen. A five-year-old girl and her parents had stopped for some ice-cream and when they returned from the store, their transport had disappeared into thin air. To make matters worse, there was an electric storm raging. As night came on the child was inconsolable and kept crying, 'Teddy *hates* storms. He is always frightened. He needs me. He is calling for me.'

They managed to get home and in desperation the mother called a friend who had a Teddy Bear and asked to borrow him for the night. 'Into the now raging storm we all went to get the substitute Teddy with lightning flashing all around us. She met the borrowed bear and smelled it, as all children do. And we grown-ups all waited with baited breath to see if he would be received.

'After much deliberation she condescended, "Well, maybe I can stand him for just one night," ' (I would have *slapped* her by now, wouldn't you?) ' "until Teddy comes home. But he doesn't smell or look like *my* Teddy Bear." '

The family returned home and nobody got much sleep that night except perhaps the borrowed Teddy. At 7 am the phone rang and it was the police telling the mother that the car had been recovered.

'Oh, thank God,' she said with relief, 'is the Teddy Bear in the car?'

'Lady,' said the policeman with ill-disguised disgust, 'we only get back fifty per cent of stolen cars intact and *you* are one of the lucky few and you want to know if there is a Teddy Bear in the car!'

Little did he know, the indulgent mother reported to me, that the Teddy Bear was more important than the car. In fact he *was* still there.

Two cris de coeur which one can only hope had happy endings: the first from the Personal Column of *The Times:* 'Lost in Cadogan Square Gardens a tired but much loved Teddy Bear.' The other from a notice board in a store at Malibu, California: 'Small brown thirty-year-old stuffed bear. Lost on La Costa Beach. Reward.'

So many of the losses seem accidental and yet have far-reaching effects on what can only be described as the loser. Peter Noel Knost, for instance, who has DDSTD after his name (what could the letters stand for?) reports 'an accidental loss during a thorough housecleaning of my three old friends, Jack, Billy and Andy'. He admits that he is now forty years old but has spent many hours reflecting on the whereabouts of his childhood chums. He even went so far as to enclose two poems on the subject. And just before you all burst into tears, Doctor (one of the letters *must* stand for that) Knost in his postscript adds, 'Since my tragic loss, I have compensated by acquiring no less than thirty Teddy Bears of various sizes.' So there!

But not all losses *are* accidental and here we go on to a purely psychological tack. There are two cases of man or rather teddyslaughter which have come my way recently. A very attractive young American lady came into the shop the other day and saw an old copy of *Bear With Me* lying around. She launched into a fairly ear-boggling story about deliberately 'killing' her old bear when her parents, who were obviously Teddy Bear snobs, gave her a brand new one. She said she hadn't thought of the incident in years and suddenly she was struck with genuine remorse.

Another tragi-comic case I know of is that of a little girl who took her Teddy to Portugal on a family holiday. On the beach, she decided that her friend, with all that fur, was suffering from the heat. She buried him in the sand so that he was protected from the sun. Needless to say, when she returned in the evening to take him home, the tide had carried him away to a watery grave or, at best, an arctophile mermaid.

The aforementioned 'snob' aspect has been the cause of much heartbreak. I am reminded of a small boy aged five who returned to America from Europe aboard a ship scheduled to dock in New York. He had in his possession a filthy old Teddy who was a constant embarrassment to his mother.

'I could not bear to let him land in New York with that horrid toy,' relates Mrs Dillon. 'So, when an opportunity presented itself, I eased the Teddy overboard into the Atlantic. My son is now thirty-eight years old and a major in the US Air Force. But he still grieves over his drowned Teddy Bear. I once even heard him tell his own children to "watch out for your grandmother! 'Cause she'll get rid of your Teddy Bear for you!"'

And this is the place, I think, to tell you of Pauline Clowes's traumatic experience and what might well be regarded by a psychiatrist as a test case.

Pauline had a companion called Tiddy whose function in life was to take all sin and blame from her young and wicked shoulders. He listened wisely to her woes, consulted with her as to what to do with her day, etc, and she, in return, wore him to a frazzle with loving. Her mother made socks and shoes of pink gingham, sewed a jacket of plaid and little brown pants over the leaky fur and patched his moulting ears.

When her fourth birthday approached her loving parents decided to extend the family budget and went out and bought for Pauline the biggest, fanciest, handsomest bear they could find. Happy and secure in the joy of the surprise they had planned for their little one, they removed Tiddy from beneath the dining-table (his usual lair). Pauline even remembers a little song which went:

> Teddy Bear has his lair
> Underneath the dining chair
> Pray take care, don't go there . . .
> Or you'll get an awful scare.

But for once Tiddy was not in his lair and in his place was this enormous new *Stranger*. Tiddy was at once disposed of, so there was no turning back.

'I still smart at the recollection of that tragic night,' wrote Pauline. 'I wouldn't even touch the interloper Biggie, as he was christened, I cried myself to sleep for many nights. Biggie never had a chance. He hung around my home for a few years, even got to sit on my bed once in a while, and then was given the heave-ho. Today of course I would be so pleased to have Biggie in my collection because he was sort of distinguished, I suppose, and he had "the hump". But I've never become quite reconciled to the loss of my talking companion, Tiddy.'

So many parents don't seem to realize the extent of the involvement of children with their toys and the dangers of tampering with any such relationships.

'To children, Teddy Bears, to whom they become attached over many years, are much more than inanimate objects and an ill-advised and abrupt separation may have as serious an emotional effect as the death of a close friend.' So wrote a lady from New Jersey and she certainly wrote with truth.

An anonymous British-born gent, now living in America, told me that he hadn't spoken to either of his parents for twenty-five years because they had thrown his Teddy into the fire at the age of seven. I mean this chap was seven. The deceased was five. His father had done the dreadful deed himself, egged on by his mother, to punish the boy for some small misdemeanour. The effect of this incident on the boy was such that he saved up all his pennies and, when he was eight, bought a new bear. This he carefully (and wisely) kept from his parents and the bear survived to accompany his owner through his studies at Oxford, doubtless assisting him to get his degree. Subsequently they marched gallantly through the German lines at the end of the Second World War. He assures me that his children's bears are fully protected against any eventuality!

One of the most frequent and dangerous ways of trying to wean a child from a beloved toy is by suggesting that they give it to a less fortunate and/or younger character. A lady from New Jersey observed that one of her four grandsons was told by his mother to surrender his friend when he was ten years old. He did this apparently without making a fuss, but it was noticed that from that moment he became mean and belligerent. 'Could there be a possible connection?' asks my correspondent, a trifle naively. Yes, dear lady, there could.

In fact I wouldn't be writing this book if I hadn't had a body blow delivered to me about fifty years ago when I came back from my public school, hoping to find my friend safely lodged where I had left him. And guess what? My mother had given him away to a jumble sale. I couldn't show my full rage, horror and misery at the time, as I was sixteen and had three elder brothers around, but, dearly as I came to love my mother in later years, it took me a long time to forgive her for that one.

Mark you, things have changed so much that these days it might be considered the height of chic to take a very old Teddy back to school. It certainly would in some of them. The other day I went down to Bryanston to give a talk to the boys and girls there. After disposing of my theatre life, my naval life and my astrological ditto, I embarked on the Teddy Bear motif. Noticing a great many older scholars in the audience, I gave them the opportunity of leaving the hall before they threw up. Nobody left, and judge my amazement and pleasure when at least three-quarters of those present held up their hands when I asked how many of them still had their Teddy Bears.

I know a young gent, who had to all intents and purposes discarded his Teddy in favour of a dog. I say 'to all intents and purposes' because the bear had been placed high on a dresser and not touched or moved in years, though we can only hope that a little light dusting or brushing of fur would have been carried out from time to time. However, four years after the dog came into the boy's possession, it was killed. On the night of the tragedy, when his adopted mother went to tuck the little boy in, there was Teddy back again, snuggled up in bed with his friend.

On the other hand, exactly the opposite type of situation arose in the home of Mrs Marty Simmons, who had a bear called Georgie. He suffered an untimely end when her dog ate up his insides. She does report that the dog got very sick but, as she pointed out, 'that didn't help Georgie much.'

I was pretty keen on Mrs Marty Simmons, whom I thought was a gentleman at first, owing to her signature and because I remembered a film about a butcher called Marty. Mrs Simmons rebuked me mildly for my mistake, saying she, as a matter of fact, was a she and 'had been for quite a while'. She affirmed that her children had never got hung up on bears, only blankets, and suspected that it was something to do with the late Georgie's unfortunate experience. She did state however that, in her opinion, if one must have traumatic experiences, it was better to get involved with Teddy Bears than an Oedipus-type relationship.

'At least bears can be avoided,' she wrote, 'but I'm not so sure about people.' She concluded one of her communications by asking me, I thought rather irrelevantly, if I was going to include informative footnotes on baby dolls who wet their beds. Let me take this opportunity of informing Mrs Marty Simmons and anyone else remotely interested that I am not.

But even more cruel than what that dog did to Georgie is the sort of thing that children do to each other. A six-year-old Teddy-owner was forced to watch his brother, curious to know what was going on inside the animal, take it to the basement and chop it up with an axe. Thank you, Lizzie Borden.

A now mature lady has very definite feelings about her younger brother who, when he was two years old and 'a regular terror', took her bear, Lordship by name, and after lifting the lid off an outside drain, dropped him down it.

43 Tony Hancock

44 Jill Bennett

45 Shirley Temple

Although her father fished Lordship out, his straw stuffing was soaked and ruined. His owner had to watch him end his life in a dustbin.

'I've never felt particularly fond of my brother,' the letter ends. Surprise! Surprise!

I know another lady who probably doesn't absolutely adore hers either. Now in her sixties, she is still haunted by the memory of what he did to her lovely big white Teddy. He, being younger, had a small brown one. One day she couldn't find hers anywhere, and, while looking for it, her mother started sniffing and wondering what could be burning. There wasn't a sign of the brother around and when her mother opened the oven, in which she was baking, there was Teddy, burned almost to a cinder, with all his lovely white hair singed.

Cousins, it would appear, can be even more lethal. A small girl visiting her slightly older relations with her own small brother, found them all ganging up on her. One of the things the little beasts thought up was to bury her Teddy Bear, having convinced her that she was too big to have one. They swore her to secrecy, assuring her that they would treat her like one of themselves (i.e. grown-up!) if she would go along with their scheme.

So she had to watch her beloved friend being packed into a coffin and put under the ground. Her innate shyness was such that she felt unable to tell anyone about this horrible experience, but many years later she dug up the spot. The only recognizable signs were the poor little fellow's shoe-button eyes.

Another young lady who won't forget a cousin in a hurry was at a family gathering in her own home and had unwisely left her Teddy lying around. One of the male cousins asked if he could have him. She naturally refused but it seems that all the adults at the party started telling her what a big baby she was. I must admit that she was sixteen at the time but that's not the point.

She eventually let them browbeat her into giving the bear up. She didn't sleep a wink that night and she determined to get him back at all costs. Unfortunately she couldn't get to her cousin's house till the end of the week. When she arrived, she couldn't see her Teddy anywhere and finally asked for him outright.

'The answer I got made me physically ill, but it seemed that two of the boys had kicked him around until the stuffing fell out and my aunt had thrown him into a dustbin. I tell you, Mr Bull, only a Teddy Bear knows how I felt and still feel till this day. I felt as if a human being had been brutally murdered and I had been responsible.'

I was quite horrified last autumn to see children collecting for Guy Fawkes Day and presenting effigies of the parliamentary assassin in the form of Teddy Bears. The poor dears were wrapped in totally unsuitable and degrading garments and I can only pray that, when the Fifth of November actually arrived, the money collected had been already spent by the little beasts or some member (human) of their families had been substituted for the bears at the last moment.

86

But I know of several cases where the unthinkable has been perpetrated and Mr Howard Shepherd, a well-known lover and doctor of Teddies and dolls, told me a sickening story. When he was seventeen, he was a Sunday School teacher at a Mission and was still devoted to his Teddy, a childhood companion, who had seen him through illness, sadness and joys.

Mr Shepherd's sister, twelve years older than himself, arrived on a visit with her small son, to whom he was godfather. He was appalled when their mother called him aside and 'made the most preposterous suggestion I had ever heard from her'. It was that he should present his Teddy Bear to the nephew. Did a Christian young man of his age really want an old Teddy Bear? she argued.

'Very much indeed, if only my mother had realized,' wrote Mr Shepherd. 'But when you stand nearly two foot taller than your mother, and that mother puts all her Cockney scorn into calling you a great big booby, you begin to find your powers of argument ebbing.' He handed over his friend to his godson and was aware of a sense of betrayal, particularly at night time when he gazed at the empty space on top of the chest of drawers in his room.

The following Easter he spent a holiday with his sister at her home, and one spring day his godson came to him in the garden and requested a story. Temporarily at a loss, Mr Shepherd, to gain time, asked his nephew to fetch his Teddy. The boy looked blank and said he hadn't got one. Mr S. reminded him of his gift but the little boy was adamant, and couldn't even remember how he and his uncle used to sit munching biscuits and every now and then giving the Teddy a bite.

The sister came into the garden at this point and asked what they were talking about. After the situation had been explained to her, she also denied that her little son had ever had a Teddy. When cross-questioned by her brother about his gift the previous year, she said with scorn in her voice, 'That old thing, we burnt that on a bonfire for a Guy last November.'

Mr Shepherd will never forget the horror he felt at that moment. 'I was out of the garden and upstairs to the room that had been allotted to me, and there on the bed I cried and mourned my old and beloved friend who had shared so many adventures with me and had now met this terrible and ignoble end.'

He bicycled away home as soon as he could, but the memory is still with him. 'Other Teddy Bears now live with me, some of them older than myself, gifts, rescues from dustbins and lonely Teddies bought from second-hand dealers. Unashamedly I love them all, and there are times when a shadowy figure of a Teddy creeps quietly in and sits with them, and I know Old Ted is still with me in spirit. There is always a home for a lost or unwanted Teddy in my home.'

Mrs Wagstaff from Yorkshire is another person in whose heart the name of Guy Fawkes always strikes a chill note. Her Teddy was Her Pride, 'always clean and fresh and brushed regularly with my hairbrush to keep in the pink of condition'. One November day her Pride vanished into thin air and she couldn't imagine what had happened to him. Later she saw her brother Ronnie's chum, playing with something which she recognized as her Teddy's squeaker. She attacked Ronnie and demanded to know the whereabouts of her befurred friend.

'Oh,' said Ronnie airily, 'I dressed him up as Guy Fawkes, took him on a trolley to collect money and then we put him on a bonfire.'

Since this incident Mrs Wagstaff tells me that she has come to dread November 5th, and I wouldn't be surprised if both she and Mr Shepherd didn't move to the United States where this sort of thing couldn't happen. Or could it? Someone has just whispered in my ear a word which sounds suspiciously like 'Hallowe'en'.

But the most stark letter I have ever received regarding deprivation or loss of a Teddy, came from a lady whose beloved brother kept him long past childhood as a constant companion. Fifty years ago when a far too playful playmate took the bear home, shaved his head and trimmed his ears a bit, it didn't seem to worry him all that much. But later he married a wife who not only failed to understand about Teddies but was also a careless mover. The inevitable happened and one day she left Teddy behind for ever. The rot set in with the bereaved husband and I quote verbatim, 'the three-Martini lunch, long long waits in airports and too long cocktail hours before dinner, my brother became an alcoholic and two years after his loss a well-placed pistol shot ended it all.'

Nuff said!

8 The therapeutic powers of Edward Bear

If anyone had forecast fifteen years ago that one day I would not only be giving a lecture entitled as above, and to medical gentlemen at that, *and* being paid for it, I would have laughed in their face. 'Ha! Ha!' I would have exclaimed. But this is exactly what has happened twice fairly recently.

My engagement came by a circuitous route. There is a highly expert, privately circulated magazine called *World Medicine* to which I submit articles from time to time. Only doctors and chemists seem to have access to it and my own medical adviser (who shall be nameless because I don't think I'm allowed to advertise his wares but he *is* frightfully good) says I only get ill in order to pick up some money from writing about it. The editor, Dr Michael O'Donnell, is certainly indulgent. Actually I would never have heard of the magazine if it hadn't been for the fact that my old friend and fellow-artiste Richard Leech writes a regular column for it, 'Doctor In the Wings'.

I first met Richard in *The Lady's Not For Burning* fairly soon after he'd decided not to be Dr Richard McClelland any more. I hasten to add that he was fully qualified and not remotely struck off, whatever that means. Well (I wish and I'm sure you do too, that I'd never started this!), it was he who suggested to a gentleman who was in charge of a post-graduate course for doctors in Coventry that it would be a good wheeze if I went and yacked at them. This was, I have to admit, after he found out that he was unable to do ditto on that particular night. Now it so happens I have a sideline of lecturing but it's usually to Ladies in Hats.

They (LIH) are fairly easy to entertain, as I tend to give them a wide range of subjects to listen or zizz to. I switch from The Theatre, with two capital Ts, to

My Naval Life, and then it's Heigh-Ho for Astrology, How I came to build a Small House in Greece and finally Teddy Bears, but rarely in the same order.

The full horror of what I was committed to in Coventry didn't dawn on me till the day before my engagement, when a Dr Smits phoned to ask me if I was Bringing Slides. I felt a cold sweat breaking out. I said, 'No, Doctor Smits, as a matter of fact.' He said 'oh' and that was that. It was then that I realized that the frivolous carry-on I was planning to get us all through the evening simply wouldn't do and might possibly be considered in execrable taste. In a panic, I spent the evening before the lecture searching my files for case histories of the Therapeutic Powers of the Teddy Bear.

Luckily I had preserved all the original letters, and armed with these and fortified by some Dutch courage kindly supplied by the young doctors and their wives, I ascended the podium with a sort of dotty confidence.

You see, I had and have great faith in my subject, and in this chapter I will try and convince you of the efficacy of the Teddy in moments of either physical and/or mental crisis. I referred briefly at the beginning of this book to the case of the boy who was run over by a car and brought back to consciousness by the *feel* of his bear, but before I get on to individual incidents, I would like to generalize.

It is a known fact that if a clever surgeon will operate on some beloved toy animal which the child awaiting surgery has brought to the hospital with him, on his return to consciousness the patient will be more concerned for his friend than himself. Come to think of it, this applies not only to children. When I had my appendix taken out a few years ago (goodness, the poor surgeon had a terrible time even *finding* it!) I started to grizzle the moment I came out of the anaesthetic. A pretty but sharpish nurse said, 'Why are you making all that fuss? Theodore is being very brave.' She then presented my little bear to my astonished eyes. There down his stomach were about six stitches. Actually I thought he looked pretty cross; but you get my point, yes?

And in case you don't, and anyhow, think mine is a freak case, I would like to draw your attention to that of Mrs Eleanor Johnson:

'When I was five years old, I was given a beautiful Teddy just before I had to undergo a serious abdominal operation. The American surgeon (one of the famous Mixter Brothers) shaved Teddy's abdomen and with red ink made a scar similar to my own.'

A lady called Sylvia Ffinch tells a moving story about a very small pink Teddy Bear who was given to her when she was having a major operation. 'I used to hold the little thing in my hand, to help me "bear" the pain,' wrote Mrs Ffinch. She recovered and some years later was asked to visit a little girl of ten years old, who was thought by the doctor and nurse to be dying.

She took her bear (Tiglath Pileser) with her. She was met by the mother who was crying, and was told that she wasn't sure if Kathleen, the little girl, would recognize her. 'I passed through to the front room and knelt beside the bed and put the little bear into her hand, saying, "Tiglath Pileser has come to help you to get better. He helped me and now he wants to help you."

'For several days Kathleen lat at death's door but she refused to let the little bear go. The priest gave her the Sacrament of Extreme Unction, but she recovered. She brought the bear back to me in case anyone else needed him but it was she who fell ill again. She asked for the little bear which I gave her, and this time, after she got really well, I told her she could keep him. Kathleen is now grown up. When I saw her the other day, her first words were, "I have still got Tiglath Pileser. He is my most treasured possession." '

Once over the operation or illness, it is essential not to let Teddy out of one's sight. Hospitals are funny places and not like home at all. I know one boy, in bed with rheumatic fever, who felt that his companion was not getting enough exercise. He decided he should be allowed out for walks. He lowered him carefully out of the window, when no one was looking. One awful day, while the bear was out for his daily stroll, the little boy felt the string go light. He hauled it up to find that some horrible bear-fancier had taken advantage of the situation and made off with his Teddy.

Somebody who realized the importance of children having a friend with them in hospital was the late Russell McLean, who became known throughout a greater part of America as 'The Teddy Bear Man'. All through his life he had been plagued by illness and spent much of his childhood in a hospital bed himself. He remembered what the loneliness there was like and decided to do something about it. Over twenty-five years ago he approached a radio station in his native Ohio, and by good luck got hold of a sympathetic listener in Miss Easter Straker, a well-known local broadcaster. He told her his dream: to buy Teddy Bears and leave them at both of the big hospitals in Lima, Ohio, to be presented to all the children the first night they spent there, alone and terrified.

Miss Straker thought the idea splendid; the problem was how to finance it. Then the determined Mr McLean had a brilliant idea. At that time Ohio had a three per cent sales tax, and each retailer gave you a sales-tax stamp when you bought an item. To help make their tax more palatable, the state redeemed those stamps at one per cent of their face value for charitable organizations. Mr McLean thought that the project might be financed this way. His scheme was enormously successful – people sent in their stamps by the thousands and he and his wife dealt with them themselves.

Ultimately the state dropped the tax-stamp plan, but by that time the scheme was well-established and the money kept rolling in from other sources. Miss Straker has a daily TV show on which children appear and sit on a Birthday Chair. It has become a sort of ritual that the birthday child gives a dollar to the Teddy Bear Man. At Christmas there is a special drive and thousands of dollars are raised regularly through direct solicitation of viewers. Mr McLean ran the whole thing from his own home until the death of his wife. And even after his own health failed and he had to retire to a nursing home, he continued in his work. He achieved his greatest ambition when he presented his fifty thousandth Teddy Bear. Soon after this he had to give up, but a club took over, called the Greater Lima Jaycees, and have already won a State Award for their work.

I must quote from a few of the letters Mr McLean received during his magnificent lifetime:

'I didn't think much of your project at first. I thought all those children already have a favourite toy. What could a new little Teddy do? *Then I found out.* Our four-year-old child had an accident and was completely terrified at finding herself hospitalized. Then came that little Teddy at a time when nothing else would have done. Our girl is grown-up now but she still has that Teddy.'

And from a less sceptical parent:

'We are a family of nine children and would like to express our thanks for four Teddy Bears we have received so far. When our daughter, Doris, was not expected to live, she clutched her Teddy during the few minutes she was still conscious. Well, our miracle girl lived and we will never forget her Teddy Bear.'

And finally:

'My daughter was desperately ill suddenly. I never thought to grab up a toy for her until she was handed a Teddy. From you. She immediately thought only of it and hugged it almost to pieces while the doctor worked on her.'

You do see that Mr McLean knew what he was about. He certainly did a wonderful job all his life, and just before his death in 1969 I was able to send him an advance copy of the first book.

His reply was typical of his entire life. It started, 'Kind Friend' and was only a few lines long, but at the end of it he wrote: 'It has taken one hour to write this much so you see why my mail goes by the way. Forgive my neglect. I did not mean it.'

It was the example of Mr McLean which started off the organization Good Bears of the World, details of which you will find at the end of the book. Many British hospitals have already benefited from the free Teddies being distributed, and the Royal Liverpool Hospital (Paediatric Division) wrote through the Divisional Nursing Officer: 'We do nurse many children who have never had the comfort of owning a Teddy Bear. Your organization most certainly provides a wonderful service.'

The Royal Hospital for Children, Edinburgh, thanked Good Bears of the World for the 'gorgeous Teddies' and in Leeds, Roehampton, Carshalton, and many other places, the work is proceeding apace. It is not only in Britain that hospitals seem to be becoming more and more Teddy Bear conscious. My friend Irene McBrien, who has a huge and unruly den of bears in Toronto, tells

46 Sinnamon

47 Russell MacLean, the teddy bear
   man

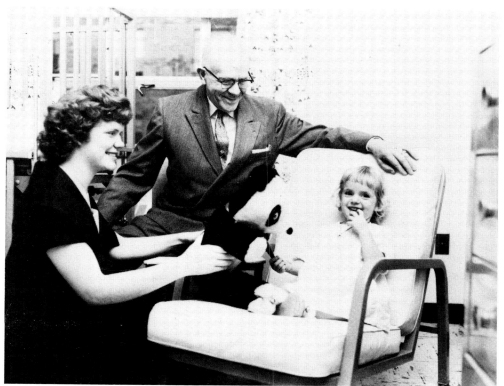

me that the Hospital for Sick Children there is festooned with bears, though mainly old ones. One of the ladies running it wrote a sad little note saying, 'Due to cutbacks by the Ontario Government we cannot afford to pay for staff, much less Teddy Bears.' However the children are actively encouraged to bring their friends to the hospital. Mrs McB was entranced to find the waiting-room walls in the Eye Surgeon's Dept covered in murals of bears engaged in various activities, *all wearing spectacles.* Naturally her own Ear, Nose and Throat surgeon has a surrealistic painting of a Teddy with a large bulbous nose in *his* waiting-room. It was this informative lady who found for me a breathtaking poster for Toronto Transports, showing Travelling Teddies.

The Dept of Recreation at the aforementioned Children's Hospital in Toronto has a five-foot Winnie the Pooh for whom a birthday party was held recently. I can only hope that he is a little less alarming than the giant Teddy in the children's ward of St Luke's Hospital, Guildford. He is called Boo-Boo and is five-foot-six in his stockinged feet, and far larger than any of the patients.

But Teddies are used for other therapeutic purposes than cheering up and companionship. Some years ago, before modern methods of inducing anaesthesia were perfected, a surgeon in Manchester asked the Merrythought Ltd Toy Factory to make a special t. bear for this purpose, by installing in it a tube connected to its mouth. The other end of the tube was connected to the anaesthetic apparatus, so, while the young patient cuddled the bear, the actual anaesthetic could be administered. Consequently the child lost consciousness without experiencing the frightening, suffocating sensations previously caused by the use of a mask. As lately as 1972 a Rupert Bear was enrolled on the staff of the Singleton Hospital in Swansea to do a similar job.

Another world into which Teddies have been plunged is that of deaf children. There is a special type of Teddy with an electronic heart which makes teaching handicapped toddlers much easier. A secret microphone inside the bear's chest carries the toddlers' voices to an electrical circuit connected with his eyes. When children speak to him, his eyes light up and flash in response. Teachers report that the children love this Teddy with the magic heart, and are learning to form speech patterns which they cannot acquire through imitation.

One miraculous life-saving story, which I can vouch for, was told me by the beautiful Eve Raphael, whose mother I once played in a television series. Don't ask me to explain that one, I have far more important stuff to write about (anyhow she was Eve Ashley then).

When her son Christopher was one year old, they had to go to New York to see her parents, and chose one of those terrible foggy periods when all flights are held up and utter chaos takes over. Flaming torches lit their way to the Terminal and days were spent in icy conditions at Prestwick and other points north. By the time they got on the plane, Christopher wasn't well at all and Eve was in a high old state. Soon after they took to the air, the little boy was delirious and on landing in New York, she carried him off the plane unconscious and stiff as a board. In fact Eve now confesses that she thought he was dead. The Captain had radioed New York and her parents were there with a doctor when the plane landed. Her mother had brought a tiny Teddy which Eve took and held in front of her small son. Eventually, he opened his eyes and, by moving the bear about and keeping him interested, it's possible she saved his life.

The next morning, to her amazement, he was jumping about in his cot, clutching his Teddy. Years later, when he went off to school for the first time, he marched into his mother's room and solemnly announced that he was leaving Teddy 'too look after her' while he was away. Teddy is by her bedside looking after her still, with a beautiful silver necklace round his tiny neck.

The Teddy Bear also becomes a security symbol when things go awry. During the war he was clutched by train-loads of evacuees, and I was amused to hear from an American lady about her Teddy Bear who came from Hamleys in London before the war. He was eventually passed on to two younger brothers. When the smaller boy heard on the radio that London had had its first bombing he clutched Teddy for his safety and exclaimed, 'But that's where my Teddy came from!'

Teddy is also a well-known antidote to tears and a bulwark against the horrors of the dark. A little chap aged seven wrote from his prep school: 'My Teddy helps me when I cry, it's from home, he's a bit old but I like him. I worry 'cause next year when I am in the big boys' dormitories they take teddies away and I shall be by myself.'

What sort of prep school can he have been in, for heaven's sake? I hope his parents whipped him out of there in double-quick time!

Dr Joshua Bierer, medical director of the Institute of Social Psychiatry in London, is a firm believer in the powers of the Teddy Bear, who, he affirms, is the only non-dangerous animal in the nursery. 'Teddies are father figures,' he adds. 'To children they represent goodness, benevolence, kindliness. Parents who replace this cosy, unharmful toy are a menace.'

Two very well-known psychiatrists in America go even further and have recently issued pronunciamentos on the need of adults to hug stuffed animals (as *they* call them) to cope with tensions.

Says Dr Rosenbaum, President of the New Mexico Psychoanalytic Association, 'A woman who lacks a man has to have something to cuddle. So she will hold a Teddy Bear, which is a lot easier to handle and doesn't create any of the frustrations that come from dealing with another human being. On the other hand attachment can be so strong that in some cases the toy' (what *can* he mean?) 'becomes part of the Eternal Triangle with married couples and causes considerable dissension.'

Another gent, Dr Markewitz, when questioned as to why so many actors and actresses get attached to a stuffed toy, said he thought it was because they tend to be more insecure than other people. The reason, he said, was that they were very often treated not as people but as commodities or pounds of flesh. He added, 'Many who feel a fantastic amount of security when they are on stage, feel much less off it.' Dr Markewitz, I disagree about the last sentence, but your heart is in the right place even if, in my opinion, your logic isn't.

There are many examples of people living under severe mental tension being helped by Teddy Bears. A man of thirty told me that he got through a serious mental illness thanks to 'his faithful and loyal friend', name of Henry. The sufferer, whom I will call John, couldn't face people or situations, and when distressed he found Henry 'a great help'. Completely recovered, he went to work in children's homes, where he again proved the therapeutic powers of the Teddy.

A lady from Maryland says that her bear, Collins A.A. Bear Esq, is very much a 'working bear'. Through four years of very serious illness he was 'my most loyal friend' (how often the adjective 'loyal' crops up when people talk about their Teddies). 'Many was the night he spent caring for me,' the lady went on. 'Now that I've returned to my vocation as a physiotherapist he has joined me in my work whenever he can.'

A correspondent from Southsea has been so comforted by her Teddy throughout her life that she longs to do something for bears as a 'thank offering'. In a long saga of sadness she reports that, 'He comforted me and was my confidant through an unhappy childhood when I was considered a difficult temperamental child. He saw me through bereavements, many troubles, and more recently through the mental troubles I still suffer after a nervous breakdown. I am picking up the pieces and trying to find hobbies and interests in life. Any ideas on how to involve Teddy Bears in my recuperative programme or do good in some way involving them? If only I could have a job connected with them!'

A lady in her late teens confesses that her bear is, 'Something like God except everyone has God and only I have my Teddy Bear. Teddy doesn't take the place of God. It's just that God knows I'm weak and need something material to love and trust in. I think he makes me easier to live with. Instead of having my emotions bottled up inside me I tell Teddy my sorrows and together we work out a solution. I think he is one of God's most wonderful creations.'

My friend Mrs Hadley, who featured in the *Life* magazine article about my book and Teddies in general and particular, is very moving about Sinnamon, now in his seventies. Mr Hadley has been desperately ill for many years and his wife has given me permission to quote from her about the situation.

'If it weren't for Sinnamon, I don't think I could keep going here alone in the house. We talk to each other numerous times a day. I don't dare change his knit-suits too often as I don't want to take the chance that his head might suffer. Not long ago I rolled over in bed and accidentally detached Sinnamon's nose. I burst into tears. I hate to stick him with a needle. He may not feel it but I do. To me Sinnamon is human.'

Again and again there is evidence that a state of mind can be improved by the companionship of a Teddy: he has a steadying quality about him which must influence the owner. His placid acceptance of everything, and his serene composure, which has no smugness about it, can often bring a sense of proportion back. You can't imagine him running for a bus or a train, can you, or getting furious at the minor irritations and frustrations of modern living.

In concluding the evidence on the efficacy of the bear's healing powers, I shall toss out three wildly different cases, in two of which he saved lives beyond any shadow of a doubt.

A German child fell from the fourth floor of a building, clutching her Teddy. She fell on top of it, breaking her fall, and only suffered minor injuries.

What happened to the bear is not disclosed. I wonder if he has been preserved in a glass case like the one who saved a baby's life in Hertfordshire. He intercepted a careless shot, fired probably by a poacher. The bullet just missed the occupant of a pram, who was cuddling his bear at the time. A grateful mother had Teddy embalmed for posterity.

I am indebted to Phyllis Anthony for the following story, which may be apocryphal but which I think has a ring of truth about it.

'I remember a story I once read as a child. It told of a little boy who was blind. There was a slight chance that he might see again but his mother, a widow, had no money for the operation. Then one day a friend of the family heard about a famous doctor in the next town. The little boy's mother decided to take him there just to ask his opinion.

'The mother explained that she had no money, but the doctor insisted on doing the operation. When the day came, mother, little boy and battered old Teddy, with one leg gone and only one eye, arrived. Next day the operation was completed. Then there were the days of waiting with Teddy beside him.

'Finally the day arrived for the bandages to be removed. The little boy looked around and first saw his mother and the doctor. He said, "You are beautiful Mother." Then he looked at Teddy and said, "Even dear old Teddy is beautiful, isn't he?"

'The day came to leave the hospital and he gave the bear to the doctor for payment for making him see again. When the little boy arrived home, there was a large package waiting for him and inside was a beautiful new Teddy.

'But in the doctor's office on the wall under glass is the little boy's Teddy with this inscription underneath:

"The largest fee I have ever received for services rendered."

9 Literary bears

'I knew Sebastian by sight long before I met him. That was unavoidable for, from his first week, he was the most conspicous man of his year [at Oxford] by reason of his beauty, which was arresting, and his eccentricities of behaviour, which seemed to know no bounds. My first sight of him was as we passed in the door of Germer's and, on that occasion, I was struck less by his looks than by the fact that he was carrying a large teddy-bear.

'"That," said the barber as I took his chair, "was Lord Sebastian Flyte. A most amusing young gentleman."

'"Apparently," I said coldly.

'"The Marquis of Marchmain's second boy. His brother, the Earl of Brideshead, went down last term. Now he was *very* different, a very quiet gentleman, quite like an old man. What do you suppose Lord Sebastian wanted? A hair-brush for his teddy-bear; it has to have very stiff bristles, *not*, Lord Sebastian said, to brush him with, but to threaten him with a spanking when he was sulky. He bought a very nice one with an ivory back and he's having 'Aloysius' engraved on it – that's the bear's name."'

Aloysius plays quite an important role in Evelyn Waugh's exquisitely evocative novel, *Brideshead Revisited,* and in a recent paperback edition appeared on the front cover.

Not that that's anything new for Teddy. He's on the front of *Ask Agamemnon* by Jenni Hall, which was a sort of incestuous thriller subsequently made into a film called *Goodbye Gemini.*

The Teddies of fiction, drama and film are not always as endearing as their image. Often they appear as symbols or alter egos. John Osborne's *Look*

98

Back In Anger uses bears as a sort of desperate therapy. The two warring principals in the play every now and then lose themselves in a fantasy of bears and squirrels.

'One way of escaping everything,' says poor tortured Alison to her friend, 'a sort of unholy priesthood of being animals to one another. We could become little furry creatures with little furry brains. Full of dumb uncomplicated affection for each other. Playful careless creatures in their cosy zoo for two. A silly symphony for people who couldn't bear the pain of being human beings any longer. But now even they are dead, poor silly animals. They were all love and no brains.' And with that she puts the bear and the squirrel back in the chest of drawers. But it must be remembered that Mr Osborne wrote the play long before he married Miss Jill Bennett who, I am sure, would never put Sir Teggy away in a drawer.

Sometimes Teddy is even used in a sinister and alarming way. Those who saw Richard Fleischer's powerful film *Compulsion* might remember a scene where one of the young murderers sits with a large Teddy Bear on his lap. The story is founded on the true case of two college students, called Leopold and Loeb, who murdered a small boy just for the heck of it.

One of the students in this particular scene is castigating his accomplice for losing his spectacles, possibly in the very spot where the murder took place. Suddenly he turns to Teddy. 'What you think of that, Teddy? You and I work out a perfect, beautiful crime, then this "superior intellect" tries to see how many ways he can find to...'

He breaks off as there is a rap at the door and Max, an already suspicious fellow-student, comes in. After a short passage of words he makes to go but suddenly sees Teddy.

MAX: What's that for? Protection?

ARTIE: Teddy. Oh I always take him everywhere. He's indispensable.

(With a quick twist he snaps the teddy-bear's head from his body and a brandy flask is revealed.)

A more sympathetic role is taken by a bear in a play of John Patrick's called *The Curious Savage.* In this an eccentric old lady called Mrs Savage lives in a sort of home for what appear to be pretty bizarre elderly girls. On Teddy's first appearance (the stage directions indicate 'he's slightly the worse for wear') one of the other ladies (Fairy) thinks he's alive, when she catches sight of him.

She asks anxiously: 'It won't bite?' and Mrs Savage replies:

'It won't shed, lay eggs or bark. And to the best of my knowledge it's unvexed by sex. It couldn't be less trouble.'

Mrs Savage carries the bear with her everywhere. Though she is a very rich woman, she has been deposited in the home by unscrupulous relatives. She has converted all her money into bonds, which she has hidden, and the family are being driven mad not knowing where. She has, of course, hidden them in Teddy's head. Eventually the truth comes out, and everything turns out lovely for everybody except the greedy relatives. The last stage direction in the play reads: 'Only the Teddy Bear, sitting alone in a spot of light in the surrounding darkness, is seen *as the curtain falls.*' All the actors I know would give their eye (or indeed back) teeth for an opportunity like that.

Other plays in which Teddy has taken a prominent role include *Dear Octopus* by Dodie Smith who, if you recall, not only understood about bears but also Dalmations. In this he played a character called Symp, because he was sympathetic and 'we used to hug him whenever we were miserable, when we were in disgrace or the rabbits died or when nobody understood us.'

In the original production just before World War II, Symp had only one arm, but in the revival with Mr and Mrs Jack Hulbert, the director saw fit to effect a miracle cure as his lack of limb (doubtless lost in some gallant exploit) was deemed too soppy.

In *Cabaret* he is the first thing Sally Bowles throws on the bed when she moves in with the American or English author (according to which version you saw or read). Teddy, was, of course, partly responsible for the successful revival of *Very Good Eddie* and television addicts must have observed that in 'Warship' there were two Teddies on the ship's strength called Brahms and Listz (not to port) who assisted the Navigating Officer no end, to say nothing of Corporal Radar's friend in 'M.A.S.H.'.

I would like for a brief moment to tell you about an American writer of verse, whose name seems to have passed almost into oblivion. Yet, with the possible exception of A.A. Milne, he has probably contributed more to Teddy's reputation than any other writer. Come to think of it, he had two names: one was Seymour Eaton and the other Paul Piper (which he always put in brackets).

He created two characters called The Roosevelt Bears and the four volumes in which they featured enjoyed a tremendous vogue between 1906 and 1910. The books dealt with two characters, Teddy G (Good) and Teddy B (Bad), and their travels and adventures round America and subsequently the world. The illustrations (many in colour) were by Floyd Campbell, and such was their success that the drawings and captions spread to postcards, notepaper, pottery, etc. One can compare their universal appeal and use to the work of Beatrix Potter. The only trouble for me is that, delightful as the books are, the bears don't look like real Teddies. They are much more like the ones you might meet in the Russian countryside if you were unwise enough to go down into the woods one day.

It's a fact, however, that the Teddy seems to have been much slower in taking up his place in British Literature. A book published around 1910 called *The Cockyolly Bird* by Mabel Dearmer had a certain amount of success and was subsequently turned into a popular play. It contained a character called Little Edward who did a Sandman's Dance *and* a tango in it.

Tardy as was the beginning of Teddy literature, in recent years the staggering number of books on the subject is overwhelming. When Jean Wright compiled the catalogue 'Hug of Bears', it appeared that two hundred books are still in print, from those suitable for tiny tots to Margaret Hutching's splendid book from which I drew so much inspiration (I hasten to add, with the author's permission).

Many books have the same hero, and just for the record here are some of the principal characters still around. I am indebted to Brian Sibley for his concise 'Who's Who in the Bear World' from an article he wrote called 'Bears For All Seasons'.

Perhaps Number One Favourite at the moment (all right, all right, Pooh fans must wait!) is Paddington. He is the creation of Michael Bond, who first introduced the little bear from Darkest Peru, with an obsession for marmalade sandwiches, in 1965. Since then there have been years of endless confusion from catching burglars to making toffee which leave the Brown family, who found him in the first place, exhausted. Recently Paddington has taken to the television screen, assisted vocally by Michael Hordern.

There is a huge, thriving industry now under the 'Paddington' banner, and there is even 'Paddington Anywhen Marmalade, guranteed to keep a bear going under the most trying circumstances'. This product is made by Paddington Preserves near Devizes.

Which brings us to Rupert, surely the Senior British Bear of all. Thirty-six companies pay for a licence to use his name on their products (or did in 1972). With not a single grey hair on his fuzzy head, he is pressing fifty-six. But then as the *Sunday Express* put it, 'Rupert Bear and Crumpets for Tea are two of those childhood wonders which never grow old.' The latter now seem to have acquired a rather ambiguous meaning, which would, I hope, have escaped the mind of Rupert's creator, Mary Tourtel, the wife of a *Daily Express* sub-editor. She also created the world of Nutwood, where Rupert lives, and its inhabitants, Bill Badger, Algy Pug and Edward Trunk.

In 1935 Miss Tourtel's sight failed and she had to cease work. An attempt to do a photographic story job on Rupert failed miserably, and Alfred Bestall took over. A Fellow of the Royal Academy, he has continued the work ever since. He is eighty-four and has no intention of giving up. By the way, I find I haven't described Rupert, though I can't believe there is anybody in the English-speaking world who doesn't know what he looks like. He is a highly individual bear, always clothed in a red jersey and check trousers, and usually with a muffler round his neck and heavy boots on his feet. He has appeared in the *Daily Express*, every day for nearly sixty years, except on two occasions. Once when

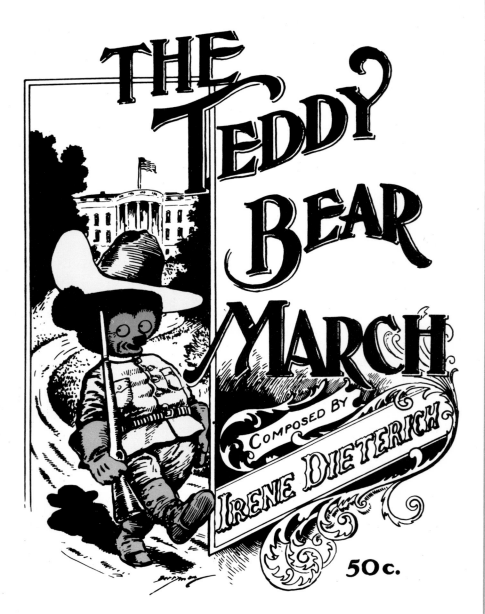

THE TEDDY BEAR MARCH

COMPOSED BY IRENE DIETERICH

50 c.

The Teddy Bears
at the Circus

he was crowded out by a Churchill speech and once by the death of Pope John.

Another typically English bear is Albert, created by Alison Jezard. He is a rather racy character who sports a checked cloth cap (and has a best one for Sundays). He lives in a basement flat in Spoonbashers Row in the East End of London, and has a small income and a grandfather clock left him by his grandfather. His best friend is Henry, a horse belonging to Mr Higgins, the rag and bone man.

Molly Brett, who does such delightful postcards for children, did an unforgettable series of drawings. My personal favourite is of a large Teddy Bears' Picnic round a camp fire. Miss Brett told me she borrowed a lot of real bears from children and kept them in her studio for a month. There was a party at the end for the owners and the bears went home with sweets in their paws.

Teddy Robinson features in several books for very young children. His author, Joan G. Robinson, gave him a string of adventures and now that he has moved from Camberwell Green to Norfolk, he looks back on his escapades with nostalgia.

Finally there are The Shoe Shop Bears who were born in January 1962, when the author Margaret Baker saw three bears earning their living by amusing young customers in a shoe shop in Taunton.

And from the book-publishing world to the song-publishing ditto. Between 1907 and 1911 over forty titles *beginning* with the words 'Teddy' or 'Teddy Bear' were registered for copyright purposes. So heaven knows how many songs in all there were, depicting the activities of the dear things.

A lady called Elsie Phelan had them 'Going Walking', 'At their Noonday Rest', 'Playing Leapfrog', 'Returning Home' and just plain 'Waltzing'. Whereas Mr (or Mrs) O'Grady had them 'At Home', 'Coming From School', 'Going to School' and even 'In School', briefly I hope, in order to take part in 'Playing Football', 'At the Dance' and 'Coming From the Dance', 'In Slumberland' and, strangest of all, 'In an Airship'.

There was a Teddy Bear March and a Teddy Trombone March, to say nothing of a Teddy Bear Rag and a simple Teddy Bear Song. There was a Teddy Bears' Dance and a Dance of the Teddy Bears, not to be confused with 'The Little Teddy Bears' Dress Ball'. Numerous titles just had the word 'Teddy Bear', or 'Teddy', and the similarity of all the songs on this theme was quite extraordinary during this period. Music shops must have become exasperated by their customers getting their requirements even slightly wrong.

For instance, should they have been asked for a song about 'Teddy and Home' they would have been faced with the following alternatives: 'Teddy's Coming Home Again', 'Teddy's Come Home', 'Teddy's Come Home Again', and the peremptory 'Teddy Come Home' and 'Teddy Come Back'. 'Teddy Come Back' and 'Teddy We're Glad You're Here' were obviously written to celebrate the traveller's return from such outposts as the jungle where he habitually went, judging from 'Teddy in the Jungle' and 'Teddy the Jungle Bogie-Man'.

In Britain the Teddies are equally active. They boogie, they dance, they frolic, they do the cake walk, they walk quite simply, they touch the ground, they get mixed up with hobby-horses and of course Have A Picnic.

'The Teddy Bears' Picnic' has, you will be amazed to hear, had a most chequered career as a song. It was originally brought out by Witmarks in New York to coincide with Roosevelt's bid for re-election in 1907. It was later published by Feldman's in London. It was played quite a lot at first by light orchestras but was soon dropped by them and relegated for use as circus background music.

In 1930 Bert Feldman approached Jimmy Kennedy to write new lyrics to the song. Kennedy, later to become world-famous as the author of 'The Isle of Capri' and other big hits, was at that time a struggling writer and went home to reset the 'T.B.'s Picnic' in his bed-sitting room. It was then used by a kiddies' troupe in a Manchester pantomime. Still nothing startling happened until Henry Hall, who had taken over the BBC musical department from Jack Payne in 1932, started looking for items for children. His manager got hold of the song which was immediately re-orchestrated and put on the air by a well-known singer of the period called Val Rosing. The response was electrifying and the BBC was swamped with enquiries and requests. Henry Hall and his own orchestra rushed out a recording, which has been a best-seller for nearly forty years and is now in its third million.

Probably the two songs next in order of popularity on the same subject are 'Me and My Teddy Bear' ('Have no worries, Have no care!') and 'Teddy Bear' sung by a Mr Presley, to which reference has already been made.

But the wittiest ones, in my opinion, were those written at least half a century ago. In the days of revue there were many numbers with a Teddy Bear motif. A popular British star of the period, Teddie Gerrard, was constantly making merry with them. One of her songs became all the rage: it was from a show called *Bric-a-Brac* produced in London in 1915.

> Everybody calls me Teddy,
> T.E. Double D.Y.
> Yankee-Swankee
> Full of Hanky-Panky
> With the RSVP eye
> All day long I telephone
> Keep repeating hard,
> Are you there
> Little Teddy Bear?
> Naughty Naughty One Gerrard.

It should be explained to the modern generation that Gerrard was once the name of a London Telephone Exchange, so the whole song becomes a sort of quadruple entendre.

Earlier still there was a delightful number from *Pelissier's Follies* in 1909.

> I wish I had a Teddy Bear
> To sit upon my Knee.
> I'd take him with me everywhere,
> To cuddle up with me.
> I'd scorn young men,
> No lover then,
> My lot in life should share
> They might go to Jericho
> If I'd a Teddy Bear.

I've been desperately trying to trace a poem or song called 'The Teddy Bear Scouts'. I am assured by Lord Butler's sister Iris that two of the lines went like this:

> They had a *famous* breakfast for a start,
> Their names were Blisters, Bullrag and Bart.

Quite apart from anything else, I must know *what* they had for breakfast!

In America at the beginning of the century it was with Theodore Roosevelt that so many of the earliest compositions were linked. There was, for instance, the Teddy Roosevelt March and Two Step and a song with a very curious lyric indeed, admonishing the President of the United States:

> Our President's a naughty man.
> He's bold and bad I know.
> He shoots poor little Teddy Bears
> My Nursey told me so.
> I'm going to write to Washington
> If you don't think I'll dare
> I'll show you, for he cannot shoot
> My Teddy Teddy Bear.

It's actually 'Nursey' who wants shooting for passing on such wildly inaccurate information. The one thing the President was renowned for in this connection was for *not* shooting little bears. Otherwise you wouldn't have to be reading all this drivel because none of this would ever have happened.

10 Three cheers for Pooh! For who?

'Pooh, looking a sprightly, if slightly bedraggled, fifty years of age sat back and contemplated the rain falling on his birthday cake.'

So wrote the *East Grinstead Observer*, reporting the first of the festivities celebrating the famous character's half century. He himself had been flown over in Person from New York specially for the occasion. The scene was set at Forstal Farm, Withyam, Sussex on June 19 1976 and was organized by Miss Joan Wood, Mrs Shirley Harrison and other Pooh-addicts, in aid of National Playgroup Week. It was in fact a trifle premature (by three months as a matter of fact) but no less than five hundred people and well-nigh double that number of Teddy Bears attended, coming from as far away as Edinburgh (Colonel Henderson in charge of that party, natch) and Devizes (leaders unknown). Had the weather been fine, the present record for a T.B. Picnic would have been beaten, but it Rained and it Rained and it Rained.

Despite the inclemency of the elements, a pilgrimage was made to the 'Enchanted Place' (Gill's Lap) in Ashdown Forest. Promptly at four pm the procession, led by Montreal Ted (our Olympic Games mascot) carrying Pooh, wound its way down from the farmhouse to the field by the lake, in the centre of which was the Hay Cart, on which had been set the tea table for the birthday party. Amid loud cheers Pooh and his friends took their seats round the table. Among them were modern reproductions of Tigger, Eeyore, Piglet, Kanga and Roo, Rabbit and Owl, though the latter stayed wisely in his tree house throughout the afternoon. Other distinguished guests included Rupert, Paddington, Gwynedd Rae, the eighty-five-year-old author of the 'Mary Plain' bear books and Brian Sibley, the walking, talking, Pooh, Milne (and incidentally

Lewis Carroll) Encyclopaedia. The Teddy who had been awarded 'The Jet Setter Bear of the Year' title for his travels round the world with a local Hartfield air hostess, popped in and two local sisters brought two pram-loads with twenty-six bears squashed inside.

The crowds sang 'Happy Birthday' to Pooh who seemed Pleased At It All, and then the huge birthday cake was broken into pieces and given to all the children and animals present. Then all who could find space climbed into automobiles and drove up to 'The Enchanted Place'. Here Pooh, with some physical assistance from Miss Jan Hopcraft, the indefatigable publicity lady from Methuen's Children's Books, planted an oak tree to commemorate the occasion.

In conclusion Pooh sat on the ground, carefully guarded against the damp, with his back to the centre tree and everybody crowded round in a circle, while Mr Sibley read the closing chapter from *The House at Pooh Corner*. There was a repeat performance of 'Happy Birthday, dear Pooh, Happy Birthday to Yooh', followed by a rendering of 'The Teddy Bears' Picnic'. It was an impressive ceremony and all the participants retired damp but delighted.

A fortnight later there was another Pooh anniversary ceremony near Faversham in Kent, where a Teddy Bears' Picnic was the main attraction at the Ospringe Church Fete. This time the sun smiled and two hundred bears turned up. The only thing which would have marred it for me was the consumption of numerous gingerbread biscuits and jellies in the shape of bears. Ugh!

But the elements were again extremely unkind on October 14 1976, when Messrs Methuen themselves organized a second jamboree. This was in their eyes the official date of Winnie the Pooh's fiftieth birthday, though Christopher Robin Milne violently disagreed. 'Pooh isn't fifty,' he told Miss Jean Rook of the *Daily Express*. 'I had him when I was one year old, so he's fifty-five. I'm appalled and I think my father would have shuddered at all the fuss.'

I will enlarge on this later. Suffice to say that Christopher Robin did not attend the junketings at Cotchford Farm (the Milne residence in the country) nor indeed did Winnie the Pooh, who had returned to New York, where he had to fulfil his social commitments which included a party in the Bronx Zoo. I, on the other hand, was delighted to accept the publishers' invitation, which I expect had been dished out because on the previous day I had taken part in a BBC radio programme entitled 'Three Cheers For Pooh!' This was written by the afore-mentioned Brian Sibley, whose script was witty, economic, amazingly untwee and in fact a model of its kind. We were also lucky in having John Tydeman to direct it, and the services of Norman Shelley to recreate his unique and ravishing impressions of Pooh, Eeyore and Piglet. The BBC had celebrated the birthday fairly continuously with readings by Bernard Cribbins from Pooh, and a television documentary entitled 'Mr Shepard and Mr Milne'.

The Methuen party was organized up to the hilt and the wine and food delicious and plentiful. But I'm sure that had nothing to do with the vast coverage given the occasion by the journalists present.

Only a small percentage of us Pooh lovers caught influenza from playing Poohsticks in the torrential rain. For the uninitiated, this is a game invented by Pooh some fifty years ago and consists of the players dropping sticks into a stream one side of a bridge and rushing to the other side to see whose stick comes out first, if you know what I mean. Or perhaps I should say, if you follow my drift. I chickened out of all this but I had already done my duty by being filmed carrying crates of wine into the Enchanted House and I think disappearing into the Enchanted Loo. Southern Television captured this immortal sequence but I hope it was cut from the edited version. Though I escaped influenza I think I was lucky not to develop a hernia, as the wine had to be transported from the coach which had naturally got stuck in the mud not very nearby, and was captained by a not entirely Pooh-minded driver, who could be described as a Pooh-Cross-sticks.

Apart from him, it is very difficult to imagine an anti-Pooh Minority Group because all the Poohaha surrounding the recent celebrations, has proved his universal appeal throughout the last half century and indeed throughout the entire world. But how then, you may or may not ask, did it all begin?

Well children, and above all, adults, like this. An extremely pretty young lady called Daphne Milne went into Harrods one day and bought a Teddy Bear for her son's birthday. Why she chose this particular one is a mystery but fifty years later Christopher Robin put it very neatly in his book *The Enchanted Places*.

'A row of Teddy Bears sitting in a toyshop, all one size, all one price. Yet how different each one is from the next. Some look gay, some look sad. Some look stand-offish, some look lovable. And one over there has a specially endearing expression. Yes, that is the one I would like, please.'

The bear didn't know it at the time but he was to have an astonishing future. As Brian Sibley in his radio script put it, 'Some Bears have Greatness Thrust Upon Them.'

In 1920 A.A. Milne was thirty-eight and his wife, Daphne, about ten years younger. He was a successful playwright and journalist, modest, gentle, bubbling with a quiet stream of bizarre humour. This humour, we are told, began to flow around the fat furry shape of the gift from Harrods.

One day young Christopher Robin Milne came down from the nursery when Sir Nigel Playfair, a whimsical and distinguished actor-manager of the period, was in the sitting-room talking to Mr Milne. In a gruff voice the boy said, 'What a Funny Man. What a Funny Red Face.' When rebuked for discourtesy he denied speaking the words himself. He said it was his bear, whom he called Pooh, speaking.

Let Christopher Robin himself continue the story:

109

Huw Woodmaman

I am theodres Brother I have come for the week.

Benson School
Shirley 5-12-72
Dear Mr Bull Thank you very much for coming to talk to us about Teddies on Friday and listening to our service We hope you enjoyed it and had lotes of fun listening to it Best of all I liked crochery and the smallest Teddy Bear in the world also I liked Theadare he looked very worm and cuddey I liked all the Tedd Bears furneure and the piano Thank you again for coming From Huw Woodman and Pandy

Benson School
Shirley 5-12-2
k you for
very much
is listening
and Crovchery
owy and I hope
well and
a cold
ve, I hope
ked our
service my teddy Bear
is callid Bumps because I
like throwing him down the
stairs but his arms and
legs are falling of and
I take him to bed with
when it is cold but in
the summer I make his own
bed
from
Jason and Bumps
Drake

My Teddy
My Teddy bear had a
Friend, His name was
Rupat, We had nice games
together. But at night
he woke me up and we
played with the toy soldiers
and the toy Farm and in
the morning he woke me
up again and I got dressed
and went down to breakfast
with them
THE
END

MARK A Jackson

Benson school
Shirley
5-12-72

Dear Mr Bull, I liked your
talk very much, please tell
Theodore and Snowy and
all your other bears that
I am glad they came to
see us. I liked Crotchety
best I think it was a
good idea to call him
that because he was
crocshad. I hope I see
you again and I hope
I will see you in Alice
and wonder band and
you are the Duchess. I
am glad we bought you
a pen as you lost yours.
I liked it when you took
them on a plane and you

Andrea Matthews   Rupert the bear

Linda Wilkie
£ lyt
The
Panda

Dear   Mr
for   comes
our   Servi
liked   ver
I expect
the   other
teddy   would
see   Theax
the other of your teddies
again. My   teddy can almost
remember   when I though
him   in   the fire
luckily   my dad got
him out or he would
of been burit to
smithereens funny thing is
just after that his
head dropped off luckily
my mums going to sox
his   head on. P.T.O

asked the hostess to
do up their safety belts
and the hostess got fright
ened and I liked your
stories about the bears.
The big bear I've forgotten
his name but he was
about the size of my
brother who is siz y
am very glad you came.
                lots of love
                Andrea Matthews
                    and
            Rudlf and Ruily
                    xxxx
PS love to Teodore and
other teddies and happy
christmas to you all

'Gradually he began to come to life. It started in the nursery; it started with me. It could start really nowhere else, for the toys lived in the nursery and they were mine and I played with them. And as I played with them and talked to them and gave them voices to answer with, so they began to breathe. But alone I couldn't take them very far. I needed help. So my mother joined me and she and I and the toys played together and gradually more life, more character flowed into them, until they reached a point where my father could take over.'

Thus Pooh came into being (in the early days he was plain Edward Bear) along with the boy's other toys. A piglet (brought by a neighbour), a stuffed donkey, a kangaroo and offspring and a tiger. Adult visitors, on being invited, would ask, 'I suppose Pooh will be there?' Milne started writing about Pooh. His wife recalled, 'We were all acting little incidents with Pooh and the nursery animals the whole time...we were all quite idiotic about it. The animals had become very important to us.'

Mrs Milne says they had fun in a world of special intimacy, laughing at ridiculous jokes and 'talking in our own special language. Looking back to those days, I always see Pooh and the small boy with whom we shared them... with his large brown eyes and beautiful corn-coloured hair cut square.'

'Yet is this the whole story?' asked the late Robert Pitman in a brilliant and exhaustive study of the subject in the *Sunday Express* of June 26 1966. In this he revealed what Christopher Robin thought of it all, in an article called 'Father' which he wrote in 1952 at the age of thirty-two.

'Strangely enough, though my father wrote so much about me, he did not like children...in fact he had as little to do with children as possible. I was his only child and I lived upstairs with my Nanny. I saw very little of him. It was my mother who used to come and play in the nursery with me and then tell him about the things I thought and did. It was she who provided most of the material for my father's books. As far as I can remember I knew nothing of the stories until they were published. Then my Nanny used to read them to me.'

'Was the son being fair to his father?' asked Mr Pitman. 'We know that as he grew older the boy hated the idea of being the Christopher Robin of the stories and was constantly being teased about his Teddy Bear.'

Christopher Robin himself, possibly since the death of both his parents, seems now able to look back with detachment and truth, and I quote again from *The Enchanted Places*.

'My father, who had derived such happiness from his childhood, found in me the companion with whom he could return there. But with Nanny in the way he could only take his dream son and return in imagination. To mend a train or keep a dormouse or go fishing. When I was three, he was three, when I was six, he was six. We grew up side by side and, as we grew, so the books were written. Then, when I was nine and he was nine, Nanny left. We could now do real things together: reality could in part replace the dream. For the next nine years we continued to grow up alongside each other. I was not aware of this of course. I just saw him as my father...I needed him. He no less, but for a different reason, he needed me to escape from being fifty.'

Afterwards the relationship deteriorated, and part of it was due to the continued success of the books about him and Pooh. 'If I had been a different sort of person there would have been no problem. Unfortunately the fictional Christopher Robin refused to die and he and his real-life namesake were not always on the best of terms.'

Christopher Robin Milne has spent the past twenty-five years in comparative but reasonably contented obscurity as a bookseller in Dartmouth, Devon, trying to live down his childhood and irritated by customers who want to bring That Subject up. Only recently has he seemed to come to terms with it all, and he describes *The Enchanted Places* as a kind of personal catharsis, as it was intended once and for all to tell the story of the real Christopher Robin. His next book, another autobiography, will not, he assures us, mention Pooh or his childhood.

But let's get back to Pooh and at least half the reason for his lasting attraction. Namely the work of the artist who brought him to visual life, Ernest Shepard.

'He came along,' said Christopher Robin, 'looked at the toy Pooh, read the stories and started drawing; and the Pooh, who had been developing under my father's pen began to develop under Shepard's pen as well. You will notice if you compare the early Poohs and the later ones, what it is that gives Pooh his particular Poohish look. It is the position of his eye. the eye that starts as quite an elaborate affair level with the top of Pooh's nose, gradually moves downwards and ends up as a mere dot level with his mouth. And in this dot the whole of Pooh's character can be read.'

But without belittling Shepard's invaluable contribution, it seems to me there is far more to the mystique than that. A.A. Milne caught in some mysterious way a style which was to enchant not only juvenile readers but also adult ones. Mr Alderson in *The Times* put it pretty succinctly: 'The neatly turned stories, the felicitous humour which works so well at adult level and child level alike and above all the dialogue – the changing tones and phrases which body out the characters of Pooh-and-Piglet-and-Owl-and-Rabbit, and lugubrious, sarcastical Eeyore.'

How else can one account for the success of the work all over the world? It has been translated into twenty-two languages (including Esperanto and the Initial Teaching Alphabet). Over ten million hardbacks alone have been sold in America since 1926 and thirty-six years later it was still being reported in the *New York Times Review* as one of their top-selling children's books. In Britain the sales of the four Milne books (*When We Were Very Young,* first published in 1924, *Winnie the Pooh,* 1926, *Now We Are Six,* 1927 and *The House at Pooh*

Corner, 1928) sell annually half a million copies, of which thirty per cent are sold in South Africa, Australia and New Zealand.

I knew that Pooh was very big in the last two because reports had come in from there. Sydney University's Tiddlewinks Society (who else for heaven's sake?) organized a Pooh Festival: a programme of infinite variety, which lasted four days. A crowd of two hundred attended the opening and five hundred turned up for a Pooh reading. There was a touching lamplight farewell to Pooh on the front lawn and he then left for the University of New South Wales, where equally enthusiastic demonstrations took place. There is also a Pooh Society in New Zealand, where they play Poohsticks with real live people when it is warm weather and there are convenient piers surrounded by water nearby.

There are Pooh societies all over America and in universities there the legend is perpetuated. This doesn't surprise me in the least, remembering how Pooh became the darling of the Intelligentsia in the twenties. He had a remarkable effect on the doyens of the Algonquin Round Table coterie, including Alexander Woolcott, Harold Ross, George Kaufman, Robert Benchley, and most of the *New Yorker* contributors, who were reputedly pretty tough cookies. The sole dissentient was the diminutive Miss Dorothy Parker, who wrote the book reviews for the magazine under the pseudonym of 'Constant Reader'. On reaching page 5 of *The House at Pooh Corner,* Miss Parker announced, 'Tonstant Weader Fwowed Up'. It is reported that Mr Milne, though naturally a tidge miffed when he heard of this, had the wit to add the phrase *'sic,* if I may' when quoting Miss Parker's devastating comment.

Certainly the intellectual appeal of Pooh appears to be constant and genuine. In Britain at Oxford smug Pooh addicts read about their hero from the Latin translation, and at Hull University the Pooh Society challenged all comers to a British Students' Poohsticks and Hum Championship ('Hum' is a Winnie the Pooh Poem). In the comparatively new University of Essex, a hundred or so out of the four hundred students were to be seen some years ago gathering nightly under the oak trees and listening to Readers of Pooh, holding red and blue balloons, recounting the adventures of their hero. But who was actually holding the balloons, readers or listeners, has not been disclosed.

There were several offshoots of the educational aspect of the animal's success. Professor Frederick C. Crews published a hilarious collection of parodies, *The Pooh Perplex,* in 1963. Two of the articles are especially worthy of note because of their titles: 'A.A. Milne's Honey-Balloon-Pit-Gun-Tail-Bathtub Complex', and 'The Sacramental Meaning of *Winnie the Pooh'.* The first was written by one Carl Anschauung MD and the second by C.J.L. Culpepper D. Litt.

A slightly more genuine by-blow was a series of candid revelations in the *Church of England Newspaper* written by the Rev Christopher Idle on 'The Religious Persuasions of Pooh and his Brethren'.

114

52 David Evans with Michael his
bear and Christopher Robin
Milne

But it's time to get back to Pooh and his Literary Career. I must say it was news to me that he was named Winnie after a real-life brown bear who lived on the Mappin Terrace at London's Zoo and Pooh after a swan whom Christopher Robin had met at Angmering. But even I know what 'Ther' means. He wasn't always called by this name. It may be remembered that he made his first brief, if stoutish, appearance in *When We Were Very Young*:

> 'A bear however hard he tries,
> Grows tubby without exercise
> Our Teddy Bear is short and fat,
> Which is not to be wondered at!'

As Mr Sibley surmised in his radio histoire, 'One day after the publication of the *When We Were Very Young* verses, Pooh was discovered face-downwards, behind the ottoman, from where he was heard to announce that he didn't like the book very much. He likes stories about himself best because he's that sort of bear, and it soon became clear that he would have to have a book of *his own;* so on October 14 1926, Methuen very kindly published *Winnie the Pooh* for him.'

Not that he's known by that name in other countries. He's 'Macko Pu' to the Slovaks, 'Peter Plys' to the Danish, 'Pu der Bär' to the Germans, 'Joanica-Puff to the Portuguese, 'Nalle Puh' to the Swedish, 'Ole Brumm' to the Norwegians, 'Micki-Macko' to the Hungarians and 'Kubus Puchanek' to the Polish, who have named a street after him.

In the Russian he is not very attractively called 'Vinni-Pukh'. In this version he has learned a kind of halting Russian to match his halting English and has moved from the wonderful forest to the 'taiga'. Vinni-Pukh has become the favourite of millions of Soviet children to whom the word for Teddy Bear has always been 'Mishka'. The translator of the Milne work is Boris Zakhoder. He explains to his readers about the new name. 'Kristofer Robin knew a swan (swansdown in Russian is "Pukh Pukh") and if you call a swan "Pukh Pukh" loudly and he doesn't answer, you can always pretend you were just making funny noises for the heck of it. Anyhow Kristofer's swan disappeared so he named his bear Pukh so that his name wouldn't be forgotten.'

Zakhoder is at his ingenious best with English words which have a double meaning in Russian. For instance the word there for 'discover' also means 'open' (Otkryt). Vinni thus thinks the North Pole is a box to be opened, not a Place to discover. *Vinni-Pukh I Vse-Vse-Vse* (and all-all-all) is one of the most successful children's books to appear in Russia in the last decade; nearly four hundred thousand copies have been printed, there have been Vinni-Pukh puppets and TV shows and untold millions of children have rechristened their 'Mishkas' 'Vinni', but Mrs Milne told me it was practically impossible to get the royalties out. However she went there on a great spree to spend some of the money due.

116

There is no limit to Pooh's cosmopolitanism. In 1961 Dr Alexander Lenard produced *Winnie Ille Pu,* a Latin translation of the classic and described by the *New York Herald Tribune* as 'the status book of the year'. It took the author seven years to write the book as he had to work his way through the Messrs Juvenal, Pliny and Ovid to find sentences to fit, But over a thousand copies were sold before you could say 'Julius Caesar' and only the other day somebody told me that it was the last Archbishop of Canterbury but one's favourite bedside reading.

Nothing could stop Pooh's progress once he had taken off. During the Second World War, when shortage of materials and metal restricted the number of toys available to the small fry of the nation, Duttons, the American publishers, introduced new versions of the Pooh Stories in Pop-Up book form, an innovation which captured the children's hearts. There were also a series of variations on a theme: Christopher Robin Readers for Classroom Use, C.R. Calendars to keep the memory evergreen, Birthday books for ditto and even C. Robin notepaper. Later on we were to be inundated with C.R. smocks, Pooh Garden figures, Pooh Christmas cards, Pooh Nursery Prints, Pooh T. Shirts, Winnie the Pooh Hunny Pudding (did you know incidentally that 'Cottleston Pie' is 'Crustulum Cru' in Latin?), Silver W.T.P. Honey Spoons (just the £18), W.T.P. electronic calculators, and, whisper who dares, Winnie the Pooh underpants!

Oh yes, and there is a Pooh Get Well Book for those suffering from Wheezles and Sneezles.

Winnie the Pooh himself and his friends have managed to retain a sort of dignity, though they live a rather sedentary and cloistered life on the eighth floor of a Park Avenue, New York building, where Duttons operate. In 1947 Elliot Macrae, the president, arranged to transport the original animals to New York. Insured for fifty thousand dollars, they crossed the Atlantic and made a triumphant cross-continental tour before settling down in glass cases to receive guests in the Reception Room of the publishers. From time to time they emerge for state occasions like the exhibition of Ernest Shepard's work at the Victoria and Albert Museum in 1967, where many of his original drawings can still be seen. This wonderful artist left them in his will to the nation. I think it is unlikely that the Walt Disney films on the Pooh theme will end up in the same place.

The storm which the film *Winnie the Pooh and the Honey Tree* aroused in 1966 in Britain proved how intense and personal the Pooh cult had become. The addition of a fresh character (a gopher), allegedly to help the American market, infuriated Pooh's public and there was a fierce attack in the *Daily Mail* which stated that 'in this very Unenchanted Forest of Film Commerce, a gopher is worth more than a Piglet'. For Piglet was cut clean out of the film (although curiously left in a song) because Mr Wolfgang Reithermann, who directed it, claimed that there was simply no *room* for him. Mr R. had apparently never heard of Pooh until 1961, the year in which the rights had fallen into Mr Walt Disney's hands. Mr R. also rather unwisely announced with pride in an interview, 'as far as Pooh is concerned, we stayed closer to the original than we'd ever done on anything before.'

For three years a director, six writers, eleven animators, nine 'voices', three background artists, four layout designers and two composers had been rewriting, redrawing, and resinging the Milne book. All told, a hundred and fifty men were involved and all this for a twenty-six minute film. Only one trace of the British original remained, but just in the version shown in the Old Country. This is the voice of Christopher Robin, and it was only changed after a brave stand by Felix Barker, the film critic of the *Evening News*.

He became concerned when excerpts from the film were previewed in London. 'You might think that Christopher Robin hailed from Chicago or Atlantic City,' he wrote. 'Over the years we've grown fairly hardened to Uncle Walt's heavy hand on our nursery classics. But a nasal twang for Christopher Robin was really too much.' The accent, according to Mr Reithermann, was a Mid-West 'generally neutral accent' that he happily claimed was acceptable 'to the whole American market', the British one presumably having been overlooked.

Discovering that the film had been selected for the Royal Film Performance of 1966, Barker contacted Disney's London office and warned them if nothing were done 'we should all be waiting with our knives sharpened'. To cut a very long story short, the pressure was such that the only copy of the film in Britain was ordered back to Hollywood and C. Robin was redubbed just in time. It was disclosed later that the original voice of C. Robin was that of the son of one of the directors of the studio.

In the Shepard drawings, Christopher Robin has long hair and wears a smock. One of the American animators, Mr Hal King, commented: 'He came out too sissified. So we gave him a haircut and some decent clothes.' Actually he came out looking like Pinnochio and I think perhaps here is the place to report that a Winnie the Pooh drawing by Shepard was recently sold at Sotheby's for twelve hundred pounds. How much, I wonder, do original Hal Kings fetch?

Possibly, however, the original Christopher Robin might have been on Mr King's side all the same: 'I suggested earlier that one of the unwelcome facts that faced my mother soon after my arrival was that I was clearly a boy, and that for nine years she tried to ignore this by dressing me as a girl. I am not entirely sure how seriously I take this theory, but at least it is not out of character. Fortunately in this particular instance, mind failed to triumph over matter and I remained a boy. But only just; and I was one of her few failures.'

I cannot conclude the sad history of Pooh's trip into the film world without a

118

word about the lyrics which were supplied for his use. The delightful but unusual nuttiness of Milne's 'Hums' must have alarmed the film makers, and the Brothers Sherman (Oscar winners and all that sort of jazz!) were imported to devise an entirely fresh lot. Here for *your* opinion is a comparison:

A. A. MILNE	THE SHERMAN BROTHERS
It's a very funny thought	Oh, I wouldn't climb this tree
that, if Bears were Bees	If a Pooh flew like a bee
They'd build their nests at	But I wouldn't be a bear then.
the *bottom* of trees.	So I guess I wouldn't care then.
And that being so (if the	Bears love honey – and I'm a Pooh Bear
Bees were Bears),	So I do care – so I'll climb there
We shouldn't have to climb up	I'm so rumbly in my tumbly
all these stairs.	Time for something sweet.

The two subsequent films on the subject were *Winnie the Pooh and the Blustery Day* (1969) and *Winnie the Pooh and Tigger too* (1975), both short films. They've now been joined to the earlier one and are being whizzed round the world, I imagine, as a main feature.

Perhaps one day a film worthy of its subject will be made, but till then we can be certain of one thing. On all other fronts Pooh's appeal remains totally undiminished. As for the younger generation's attitude, it can be summed up in a phrase I heard a shopkeeper use, when asked to explain why he was always getting sold out of Poohiana. 'I can only put it down,' he said, 'to the kids wanting to be "with it".'

But the last word should, I feel, be left to A.A. Milne's two major creations, one human and one, well, almost human.

'Pooh,' said Christopher Robin earnestly, 'if I – if I'm not quite –' he stopped and tried again – 'Pooh *whatever* happens, you *will* understand, won't you?'

The above is of course from the original book. But your actual Christopher Robin finishes his moving *The Enchanted Places* as follows:

'I like to think that Pooh understood. I hope that now others will understand too.'

It should be added as a postscript that, by a discreet trust, Winnie the Pooh divides his considerable earnings between the Royal Literary Fund, Westminster School, the Garrick Club and his old friend, Christopher Robin Milne.

11 The bear facts

It is sadly true that the modern Teddy Bear has little resemblance to the early ones, and even Steiff have made adjustments to models which have seemed well-nigh perfection to me. Nowadays so-called fashionable bears wear a nylon fur coat which can be washed or brushed. A far cry from the lovely plush and velvet numbers filled with sawdust or wood shavings, who looked as if they'd seen a bit of Life with a capital L. You can now have a Teddy made of foam rubber which can join you in the bath. There are battery-driven walking bears and even one with a built-in gyroscope which enables it to ride a tiny two-wheeled cycle. There are musical bears, containing minute tape-recorders which will croon 'Happy Birthday' at you or shout out pithy remarks like 'I want some honey' or 'Kiss me'. Others will yawn and stretch when a built-in alarm clock goes off. Perhaps my most unfavourite refinement of all is the model containing a transistor-driven tape which is hidden in the bear's head. You are supposed to press a button and say anything you like. Then you press another button and the bear's eyes light up and it (I can't bring myself to call him 'he') repeats what you've told it, though the tiny loudspeaker is so adjusted that it deepens your voice into a growl. It's not advised, they say, to put this model in your bath.

I suppose some of you are saying, 'What's he carrying on about? Only a few chapters ago he was telling us about "The Growler" and other unusual bears of the early nineteen hundreds. What's the difference?'

I don't know whether I can explain, at least to your complete satisfaction. But to me there are certain things in life which should never be subjected to change if it will impair their special value, in this case security. It's simply no good having

120

a bear who gets in a bath with you (one knows instinctively that They Hate Water) or ones with machines attached to them which may give you electric shocks. Their very modernity turns them into some slightly spooky animal who is neither one thing nor the other and of whom one can never be sure. One can't imagine them listening or just Being Quiet. Friendship would seem to be out of the question because in some way they attract too much attention to themselves.

The basic security value in a Teddy used to be that they never changed in their attitude to one, and none of us older generation of arctophiles can see the point of a bear who is too intent on being clever himself to see how clever we are being. And even the ones who are so brilliantly constructed mechanically have frightfully stupid faces. Recently I've seen in shops Teddies who should be ashamed of themselves, made of some wildly hygienic washable material, shining with smugness like plastic tablecloths, and about as friendly and lovable as a hedgehog with hepatitis.

But the fact remains that there has been no startling decline in the toy's popularity since the whole thing started, and manufacturers will try to prove to us that it's because they have moved with the times. And the ghastly thing is that they are very probably right. But I can't really believe that even the most sophisticated modern child is influenced by such appeals as are perpetrated by Wendy Boston Playsafe Toys: 'Please Mummy, can we go to a shop where they've lots of lovely safe soft cuddly Wendy Boston Teddy Bears? They can go in the washing machine and through the spin dryer again and again and they last and last. They've got screwed-in nylon eyes that never come out and there's no nasty wire in them.'

The main new colours for Teddy are shocking-pink, chartreuse and orange. The original shade seems right out of fashion and I find that the actual faces have altered considerably. Yet, to be fair, I must admit that most of the larger manufacturers of the toy insist that the basic benign appearance be adhered to. He must be furry, cuddly, and above all friendly. A modern consignment arrived with eyes and mouth 'at a menacing angle' and was sent back instanter.

But as long as there is a demand for Teddy as a companion, perhaps one shouldn't cavil too much at the March of Time. After all sales are estimated at forty million dollars worth in America alone, and despite the glut of competition it's a fair bet that Teddy will occupy the honoured place on most small pillows when bedtime comes.

A recent research in America on the favourite toy for children proved a walk-over for our friend. Fifty-five per cent named him as their choice.

Mrs Hutchings supplies an enlightening report on the results of a similar survey in England. She carried it out as a result of overhearing a conversation on a bus which ended: 'What *do* children play with now that they no longer like Teddy Bears?'

This sent shivers down her spine (she was about to embark on her delightful book at the time) and in 1963 she conducted her own census on Teddy Bears. Three hundred and fifty children from the age of five to eleven were questioned, and the guinea pigs came from large and small towns, private, county, primary or grammar schools.

Fifty of the results were discarded because the children were too old or too young, or obviously had been helped. Of the three hundred kids questioned (these were all from the British Isles) only thirty (i.e. ten per cent) had no Teddy Bear: eighteen of these were boys and twelve girls. Of these, just over half came from a slum district where there was very little home life in the accepted sense of the word. In this particular area a great many of the children did not know what a Teddy Bear was. Every country child questioned, however, had one. Of the two hundred and seventy possessors, fifty-seven (twenty girls and thirty-seven boys) did not play with them. Most of these children were between nine and eleven years of age, when one would not expect a boy at least to be playing with a Teddy. (Here I cross swords with Mrs Hutchings, whose comment this is.)

The younger boys and almost all the girls added that, although they did not play with their bears, they took them to bed every night, and many of them stated that 'Bears are not to play with but to cuddle'. Of the bear owners seven children had two, three had three, one had four, and one had five and one even had eight. Therefore, less than five per cent had more than one.

Questioned about the colour of their bears, ninety-two per cent of the bear-owning children had normal-coloured bears, being variously described as brown, fawn, ginger, yellow, tan and grey. It was interesting to note that nearly all of the bears of other colours were owned by town children.

In reply to the question 'Is there anything special or unusual about your bear?' most of the children replied in the affirmative, but it was always for purely physical reasons, i.e. because they had only one eye, ear or leg or the stuffing was coming out. As the majority of Teddy Bears show the scars of war and age, this turns out to be the rule rather than the exception. In fact all seem to *enjoy* ill-health (or rather the aftermath of it). Operations become a status symbol and it is unusual to find a bear who is still in one piece.

Exactly half of the questioned children said that out of all the toys they had ever possessed, their Teddy Bear was their favourite. The girls answered a further question as to which they liked best, dolls or cuddly animals. Sixty-one per cent preferred cuddlies 'because they are lovely and warm to take to bed and cuddle'. Thirty-seven per cent chose dolls because they could be dressed and undressed and they could do more with them. Yet I suspect, myself, that by the phrase 'could do more with them' they mean have babies and all that sort of caper, but Teddies can easily perform this function, if and when required. But dolls do perform the duties of children substitutes rather more readily. Even I

122

see that. On the other hand, one of the survey's findings was that a group of older girls had admitted that they had gone back to Teddy Bears 'because I can have them sitting on my bed forever but dolls are babyish'.

But in case we are over-estimating children's regard for Teddy, it is only fair to report the findings of Doctor Geiger, a professor at a New England Medical Centre. A large group of slum children were shown a picture of one and asked to identify it. Just over 40 per cent thought it was a rat. Oh dear! Oh dear! What *are* things coming to?

I wonder what they would have said if they'd come face to face with a Thalidomide Teddy Bear with vestigial arms which came on the French market some years ago. I am grateful to Miss Ann Daubercies for this singularly unattractive bit of info. But she came with some splendid other data and a fairly comprehensive run-down on European Teddy Bear activities. There were bears with revolving eyes, twitching noses and heavy breathing, and a musical bear with a ring in its head to start off the mechanism. She also saw a chair upholstered in Teddy Bear material, the back like a bear's head and the seat forming the body. It *may* all be something to do with the fact that 'L'Ours Martin' (Martin Bear) is an unsavoury character in fables of the Middle Ages in France.

Apparently most French bears are called Martin though there is a TV programme for the very young in which they are called (or one is) Nounours. He tells stories of a rather high moral tone and then sails into the air with the Sandman, looking just like a human in a bearskin. Perhaps he is, but Miss D. doesn't think so. She just says it's frightfully unconvincing.

She was told of a French Air Force Officer who slept with his Teddy Bear, and of a friend's son (aged four and a half) who commiserated with his bachelor uncle because he hadn't got either a Teddy Bear to sleep with or even 'une petite femme'.

An Italian lady informed her that Teddies had only reached her country after the last war. Her husband had given her one, but to her a bear of any sort is cold and treacherous and the usual associations of Teddies are totally absent. A Spanish girl to whom Miss Daubercies spoke knew nothing of the animal, but a Hungarian, having to limit the possessions she took out during the uprising, managed to find room for her Teddy. Austrian bears are called 'Brum' bears because they growl 'Brum' when they move forward.

There is, without a doubt, a tendency among Latin races to be cold about Teddy Bears. As an example Miss Daubercies cites a former pupil of hers (French and sixteen years of age) who does not know or care what has become of her bear, compared with another (male, British and seventeen) who still keeps his at the end of his bed.

Rachael Feild, my British research collaborator, has a theory that Teddy Bears

123

only inspire intense interest in countries where there aren't any real ones. Austria and Germany, she maintains, are full of the Three Bears type but not the Teddy. In the wilder parts of America they don't seem half as keen on our friend as in other areas. Can it be because in the former they have to keep shooing the genuine article out of their country houses?

Yet in Russia this theory doesn't appear to work. One would have thought that a country possessing so many ferocious bears wouldn't make toys in their image. Yet here the toy bear has flourished throughout the centuries and the Brown Bear has been traditional and constant in popularity. There is naturally a strong political element in the making of things even for children, and wooden peasant and bear figures dramatize the struggle between land-workers and the primitive forces of nature.

Russian nursery lore is full of Mishka the Bear, but many nineteenth-century children seem to have called him Bruin, which joins the school of Dobbin (for donkey), Bunny (for rabbit), and Pussy (for guess what?). This makes the whole thing almost universal, as there is no doubt that before 1903 any toy bear in Britain or the United States was referred to as Bruin.

Yet the genuine article can only inspire fear, one imagines, in Russia. An animal trainer from a Soviet circus was talking on the radio recently and saying that bears were the most alarming of all beasts to work with. Lions and other animals always look cross before they attack, but bears look at you as though you were a honeypot, whether they feel that way or not. With them, as with Teddies, the expression never changes. This is important for children: it's easier to identify with a Teddy's continuously benevolent expression.

But I've news for you. Teddies can be dangerous too. Not very long ago the British Home Office issued a warning that a few imported Polish-made Teddy Bears contained a powder which could give children pneumonia. Mr Whittle, the analyst for Bristol Corporation, became the 'Teddy Bear Doctor' after this information had been received, and kept a cupboard full of the animals in his office as substitutes for the ones he had to rip apart. Well, one, as a matter of fact, for that was the sum total of Teddies found containing the fatal powder.

There is an alarming story of an almost lethal Teddy, who found his way into several people's hearts. Some years ago a Mrs Brown from Edinburgh, returning from a holiday camp, bought a large cuddly bear for her granddaughter. The wee girl loved it, played with it constantly and slept hugging it in her arms at night. Then it began to deteriorate. The arms began to tear, the seams broke open and a fine powdery spray began to burst from it every time it was squeezed. Because it was such a well-loved toy, it wasn't discarded, but patched and resewn. After a time the powder began appearing again. Mrs Brown had read something in a paper about a Home Office warning and retrieved the gift from her granddaughter.

It turns out that this Teddy (Polish-made again) was stuffed with powdered resin which had mixed with it a small proportion of wood shavings. In the powder is a toxic chemical called formaldehyde, which is extremely harmful when either swallowed or inhaled, particularly by a child. It is only fair to say that there are no more Teddies of this type on sale anywhere in Britain now, though Hong Kong imports were once believed to give off poisonous fumes in front of a fire.

And now we are on a frightfully antibear tack, and because it is only fair to give The Enemy some ammunition to combat this very long love story, I feel it is my duty to report on the recent findings of some doctors at Leeds University. They were studying 133 asthmatic children and found that mites produced the symptoms in more than half. And I know this is not the moment for a joke, but I would like to point out that those doctors didn't mean tiny mites. They meant the house pest which apparently lurks in all our homes. As if we didn't have enough to cope with already.

Anyway, these mites aren't a danger in themselves but they're found all around us, even in the most house-proud home. On clothes. On carpets. On bedclothes. On *Teddy Bears.* They don't bother healthy children at all, but when the mites die they form a dust rather in the same way as seashells disintegrate into fine sand. This dust can be inhaled from soft toys cuddled in bed. If the child is at all susceptible to allergic asthma it can set off a breathless fit of wheezing.

'Incidents' like the above provoked a fascinating survey on the Teddy Bear World by *Which?*, the magazine of the Consumers' Association. In the December 1967 issue they reported on their findings.

'In recent years some sinister Teddy Bears have been found with unhealthy insides that might well harm their owners in the latter's more carnivorous moments. So we decided to investigate "Teddy Bears".

'We have carried out post-mortems on forty, all except one of them British subjects. The odd one came from China. The bears came in all sorts of different colours, shapes and sizes, some traditional, some less so. We set out to assess how safely they were made. We tried to test the bears in their most popular sizes, from eight and a half inches to nearly three foot tall.

'Most bears had a skin of woven cotton fabric, with a pile of nylon or animal fibre. Two had woven viscous rayon, one of them with a nylon pile, the other with a viscous rayon pile. Four had animal-skin skins. All were reasonably furry.

'Like us, Teddy Bears are not the same all the way through. The stuffings of the bears were kapok, man-made fibre, rag wool flock, wood-wool or pieces of foam broken up into crumbs or a mixture of these materials. A head might be stuffed with wood-wool, arms and legs with rag flock and the body with a mixture of the two.

125

'It is important that these stuffings should be clean and that they should not contain any harmful substances that a child could suck out. The Rag Flock and Other Fillings Materials Regulations 1961 and 1965 lay down requirements for the cleanliness of some stuffings and there are proposals to cover most types. Most of the fillings we examined were satisfactory...

'Some bears had voices, usually like bleating sheep. A bear called Sonia emitted a chime and the Petkin Animated Teddy had a musical-box in its right leg that played "Hush-a-Bye Baby". To wind it up you had to twist its leg.

'Freemans Lefray TM 1560 was more conventional with a musical-box in its body and the key sticking out of its back. One of the three samples we tested played "The Blue Danube", two played part of "The Teddy Bears' Picnic" and the three Chad Valley bears with voices had them particularly well protected in plastic casings. We did not have cuddliness tested by the real experts, but it seemed to us that the Philip Winner Giant Bear and the Shanghai Dolls Factory Bear felt rather less soft in an embrace than the others.

'Arms and legs were either stiched on (the safest method of fixing them) or had movable joints...We tested the strength of the seams to see whether they were easy to pull apart in a fit of passion, or just plain curiosity. Seam strength varied quite a lot, often in one bear, but all were strong enough.

'Except for the Chinese Bear, which had glass eyes, all had plastic ones. Most of the bears had eyes fixed with washers. This is the safest arrangement, because if a child does pull out an eye, there are no wires sticking out on which it could hurt itself...

'We carried out a flammability test based on the appropriate British Standard. All except Rosebud were satisfactory; the surface of its pile burned quickly. The manufacturers tell us that Rosebud is now being made with a flameproof finish...

'We investigated whether the dyes were fast because it is important that a child should not be able to suck them out. Most of the covering materials had fast dyes, but the noses of the Petkin X913 and the Petkin Animated X220 and the paws of the Pedigree 16 J/GX were not colour fast. The body of the Pedigree 16 J/GX and the paws of the Woolworth fourteen inch Teddy Bear were not quite colour fast either.

'There often comes a time when it is necessary to wash a Teddy Bear. Some bears are claimed to be spongeable, so we sponged them. Most of the bears that claimed to be washable were washable, but some needed careful brushing afterwards to restore their looks. The nose and mouth of Rosebud Teddy came off and the Cudlam T30 suffered some loss of appearance. Tinka-Bell Teddy Bear 493's condition could only be described as 'poor' after sponging and poor Sonia chimed no more. She had started off her career with a fine chime but the current model has bells in her left ear, instead of a chime in her body.

54 & 55 Mrs Helen Henderson of Canada and
a few of the bears she has brought to life

'By and large, we can give British Teddy Bears a clean bill of health. But remember that we had not tested all the T.B.s that find their way into the shops around Christmas.'

So concluded *Which?* and I feel rather a traitor for making the whole thing so unromantic, but I think that every side of such an important subject should be discussed.

At the risk of repeating myself, I must outline the nobler aspect of the Teddy. They have gone into battle on guns, tanks and in haversacks. There is not a corner of the globe where they have not penetrated. They have saved lives by intercepting bullets, breaking falls, and just being around. They've flown round the world, been drowned in floods, burned in concentration camps and worshipped as totems. There are no cases of disloyal, treacherous or cowardly Teddy Bears. They seem destined to survive everything, and emerge as a triumphant symbol of something or other.

Miss Kathleen Lock, the chief buyer at Hamleys, insists that 'our eternal affection for Teddies is a sure sign that the British are as sentimental as ever underneath. At least a quarter are bought by the grown-ups themselves. Husbands buy them for their wives when first babies arrive, boyfriends buy them for fiancées and boys and girls smuggle small substitute Teddies back to boarding-school.'

Yes, Miss Lock, I'm sure you are right and if only I'd thought of smuggling a small Teddy back to my boarding-school, I would never have lost it in the first place or indeed be writing this book. Anyhow the following stuff concerns the two principal manufacturers of Teddy Bears, bitter rivals and referred to earlier on. Namely: Steiff and the Ideal Toy Corporation.

It must be remembered that the German firm made every kind of stuffed animal, and therefore the following instructions given out to retail shops are not exclusively for dealing with Teddy Bears.

After *unpacking*

1 *Straighten Ears*
Face Animal, place both thumbs in the ears and bring them into the correct position.

2 *Straighten Ribbon or Collar*
Ribbon or collar should not be twisted and the nametag denoting the animal should always be on the front centre.

3 *Brushing enhances appearance*
Brush short-haired animals against the lie of the plush, using a stiff bristle brush. The plush long-haired animals should be 'fluffed up' by brushing with short, brisk strokes either with or against the lie of the plush, depending on the individual toy.

Steiff animals covered with Dralon plush are stuffed with either foam rubber or Dralon fibre and may be washed with soap and water. Care should be taken however, to use warm, never hot, water and they should not be dried with heat. Complete immersion is not recommended since the stuffing retains moisture and will require a long time to dry properly.

In 1958 the German hamlet of Giengen paid a tribute to Theodore Roosevelt on the hundredth anniversary of his birth. The townspeople organized a giant Teddy Bear Festival. Carrying the blessing of the German State Department and the Roosevelt Centennial Commission, it attracted more than twenty-five thousand people from all over Europe, who crammed Giengen's cobblestoned streets. During the celebration the Teddy Bear was used by the Giengen Post Office for franking letters. Giengen has a population of fourteen thousand of which two thousand work for Steiff. Among the models they still make are the following:

The 'Original Teddy' in gold mohair and nine sizes. He is always jointed and can be supplied with a Squeeze Voice or Automatic ditto (when laid down). They offer the same in caramel mohair, and in dark brown mohair. There are also three special bears: 'Zotty', the Shaggy Bear described as 'Cuddly long-hair teddy of fine expression, jointed, super-soft, stuffed, double squeeze voice'. And then there is a 'Soft Bear Orsi, mohair caramel'. He has his head and arms jointed and is 'super-soft stuffed'. And finally, 'Lully', a mohair caramel colour with a very soft, turnable head. And as the brochure says, 'all these will withstand ferocious hugging and furious play, yet when bedtime comes they are ready to sleep quietly beside their daytime playmate, providing the assurance of a friend close by. And it all began more than eighty years ago, because the nimble fingers, lively imagination and deep love a kindly sempstress had for all children prompted her to make the World's first stuffed toy.'

Steiff claim that in 1904, twelve thousand Teddies were made for them and that in 1907 a million went from Giengen to America alone. I have no figures from the Ideal Toy Company for those years, but they are now manufacturing one hundred and fifty thousand a year. Back in 1903 they were sold by them for $3. Today they range from $2.50 to $15. To celebrate Teddy's fiftieth birthday, Ideal produced a very special one called 'The Golden Bear'.

But to celebrate their own fiftieth birthday they brought out a model of 'Smokey Bear', and for non-American readers I must explain the significance and importance of this relative of Edward's.

It is believed, and I think with good reason, that when President Roosevelt refused to shoot the bear cub in 1902, the Department of Agriculture adopted the animal as the symbol for Forest Fire Prevention and called the bear Smokey. But it wasn't till 1953 that Benjamin Michtom (in case you've forgotten, the son of the man who sent the original bear to the President), decided to court the

129

Government's permission to re-create Smokey as a toy.

Now, although other firms have been granted permission to use the bear, Ideal got the toy rights exclusively as Mr Michtom promised to 'make every kid a Government agent'. It was around this time that the whole of America had been shocked by a series of forest fires culminating in one at Montana which cost several lives. Possession of the toy immediately involves the owner in public service. With every $5, $7 or $15 Smokey Bear goes an impressive Junior Forest Ranger Badge. A few days later, Smokey's owner receives a Dept of Agriculture letter importantly marked 'Official Business'. Adults may panic but the kids love it. The envelope contains a Junior Forest Ranger registration certificate, rules and regulations and an identification card.

A special law (known as the Smokey Bear Act) was passed unanimously by the American House of Representatives and Senate giving the rights to Mr Michtom. And now hundreds of thousands of children have undertaken to prevent forest fires and to discourage their elders from abandoning campfires, and from throwing lighted cigarettes or cigar butts out of their cars. Many cities organize Forest Fire Prevention Weeks, and the windows of stores sizzle with simulated forest fires, Smokey Bears and appropriate slogans.

Now from professional makers of bears to those who do it just for the fun of it and the pleasure it gives to others. Pride of place must surely go to Mrs Helen Henderson, who is on her fifteen hundred and somethingth bear (at the time of this going to the printers). All of hers are fully jointed and many of them are really big ones. She is in her seventies and a very remarkable lady, as I discovered when I met her last year at Brown's Hotel. An appropriate venue, with its Roosevelt Room and other bear associations.

She started making Teddy Bears in 1965 and they have gone not only to children. 'To my surprise,' said this lovely lady, 'the owners comprise grandmothers, teenagers male and female, and a group of unclassifiable arctophiles.

'I make the bears out of all the modern fake furs, and one cannot tell in the piece what kind of bear you will get three hours of sewing later. As I make each bear excitement mounts. What will he look like? The head is most fun because, when it is finished, you know whether or not Teddy will have charisma. Each bear has a personality and each turns out differently. I watch in amazement the results, the angle of the mouth, the position of the eyes, and the set of the ears. Will he have charm? But I have found that, if in my opinion, he is a dull bear, someone else will think otherwise, so I never despair; I just give Teddy more time to find his soul mate.'

Mrs Henderson is from Montreal, Canada, and I look forward to having a peek at her two thousandth bear. I am sure he *will* have charisma!

Bearmakers (what a subject it would have made for 'What's My Line?' Or was

130

it one?) seem to start lateish in life. Miss Emily Scott, of Basingstoke, started in 1965 at the age of sixty-eight, and in ten years she made three thousand, one hundred and fifty bears. Hers are small and unjointed. For the first few years she worked unaided, but recently a regular helper has assisted her to stuff the bears, if I may use the phrase, and another cuts up materials for this part of the operation. The fur fabric and materials are all given her by friends in the area, and the bears are sent to recipients all over the UK and to twenty other countries overseas.

Although many have been given away, £200 in cash has been raised from the sale of bears to friends and people writing in for them, in response to her appearances with them (the bears) on TV. Miss Scott says each Teddy leaves her with a blessing for the receiver, which is the sort of service you don't always get in a shop. The recipients of her Teddies include sick folk of all ages in hospitals or at home, and many lonely old people.

The truth is that one never knows at what age one may need again the support of a childhood friend, and it is certain that the very old have almost as much reason for hanging on to him as adolescents. A letter from an Illinois lady about her mother is illuminating. In the rest home, where the old lady (she is eighty-five) lives, eight of the twelve inhabitants on the first floor have Teddy Bears with them. My correspondent ends with the shrewd but depressing observation, 'These people turn to their Teddy Bears in place of the children they have had.'

Back to Britain and the Bearmakers. Mrs Jessie Frost of Ilkley is well over her first thousand. Hers are of the knitted variety, like my Snowy made by the children of the Royal National Institution for the Blind, unorthodox-looking but wonderfully cuddly and soft.

A slightly similar Teddy was given me by Mrs Wrist who lives at Kingston-on-Thames. Mine is called Edward Ginger Nylon. Some years ago, as a result of reading Margaret Hutching's book, Mrs Wrist started making bears. She was very ingenious in her choice of material. She started off with a knitted jointed one and then made one out of a remnant of Crimplene. After making twelve cousins of Edward G. Nylon (sort of gingerbread Teddies really) she took them to a church bazaar and raised funds by their sale.

They are made as 'Flat Teds' filled with foam plastic sheet, which makes them very light and easy to hold. Several are helping in a Nursery School for physically handicapped children and are ideal for little crippled hands to hold.

The bug has bitten Mrs Wrist and she now possesses a large family of bears herself, constructed from odds and ends. The one with the most character is Hattie, made from printed fur fabric. She looks as if her mother had gazed too long at a giraffe. 'But,' wrote Mrs Wrist, 'the problem is that the Teddies are taking over. I find myself spending more time actually playing with them or could they be playing with me?'

131

Mrs Wrist has had a long affair of the heart with Teddy Bears. She was a refugee from Nazi oppression and came to this country to work as a maid before the last war. As she was a trained dressmaker she was given written permission to take her sewing machine with her, a fairly large treadle model, which she still uses to sew the Teddies. All her luggage had to be checked by a Gestapo officer and the chap chosen to supervise her packing was a most objectionable specimen. Nothing was right and he refused permission for quite a number of things to be packed and taken. Mrs Wrist is sure it was out of spite. When it came to the sewing-machine, partly packed and padded out with her eiderdown and pillow, everything had to be taken apart. As he pulled out the eiderdown, her best white Teddy Bear, named Maxie after a favourite cousin, fell on the floor, with his arms outstretched to the horrid Gestapo man, who rather surprisingly said 'All Right.' She could only imagine that Maxie had temporarily softened his stony heart. Incidentally, Maxie served with Mrs Wrist in the ATS from 1941 until 1945 and finally came to a sad end in her daughter's cot. Something, says Mrs W., to do with cod-liver oil, but she would rather not go into details.

She is now known as 'The Teddy Lady' or even 'Mrs Teddy Bears' which delights her. A few years ago she made an appeal on 'Magpie' (Thames Television) for physically handicapped children. She made a very large and round grey Teddy called Tubby specially for the occasion. The Wrists live within walking distance of the Studios but her husband refused to be seen carrying an enormous bear in his arms so poor Tubby was put in a plastic bag, suitably addressed. The Commissionaire at the Studios had no sense of humour and prodded him on arrival, after taking him out of the bag, and checked him for any protruding wires. He nearly jumped out of his skin when the bear gave a deep growl in protest. He eventually reached his destination and appeared several times on the programme looking, as Mrs Wrist reported 'very photogenic and a fine example of local bear making good'. He is now giving much love and comfort in the playroom of a holiday home for Disabled Children in Norfolk.

She recently compiled a talk which she gives at various women's clubs throughout the country. It is called, flatteringly for me, 'Of Books, Bears, and Mr Bull', and is filed in the National Federation of Townswomen's Guild under this title.

When this valuable arctophile mentioned at her family Christmas party that she was working for a Teddy Bear revival, her sister-in-law, who is a Tutor and Warden at a College of Education, said that this was not necessary, as almost every girl in *her* college had a bear on her bed.

Which is old hat to us, is it not? And if you have any old hats I suggest you send them to Mrs Wrist and see what she makes out of *them*.

12 The bears themselves

During the past decade or so, Theodore and I have become intimate with a great many bears from all over the world. His correspondence, quite apart from mine, has become very heavy, and his secretary has his work cut out to deal with both lots, which usually need a different kind of approach. Theodore finds himself not only the Marj Proops of the Teddy World, but also on the receiving end of articles of clothing, books, birdcages, grand pianos and even offers of new homes. Proposals of marriage from lady bears are not unknown, and it takes a Taurean like him to keep his head and a bossy Arean like me to see that he does.

A great many of the letters received are written through the agency of a third person (or do I mean second?). They start off with phrases like 'I happened to look over my owner's shoulder and. . .' The majority reflect the satisfaction which the writer feels in being able to express feelings or exchange confidences with a fellow creature whom the cynics would describe (totally inaccurately) as a 'stuffed toy'.

Some are openly boastful: 'I have acquired over the years a certain ebullient confidence, trustworthiness, rugged charm and, well, permanence,' writes one, who goes on in a slightly deprecating way: 'I am, it must be admitted, a replacement for an earlier companion who was handed down through the family and ended up very much the worse for wear, after eighteen years of service, in a splendid burial in Hertfordshire. He is no doubt in the happy bear hunting ground.'

The writer has travelled in some fourteen countries, as far south as the Atlas Mountains and as far north as, well, York. He is seven inches high (I mean tall,

133

of course), white with black limbs, ears, and shoe button eyes.

'My duties, apart from *being there*' (the italics are his) 'are few and not at all exacting. Apparently my positions remind my owner of some detail, something to be done, a telephone call to make, a letter to answer. On my woolly suit I have pinned a tiny perfect replica of the Evil Eye. Nothing effeminate. Just business-like. My name, by the way, is Peb, constructed from the initials of three friends.'

Sometimes a young arctophile will raise his or her bear to almost idolatrous heights. There are several correspondents who are of Royal status and Theodore and I have to mind our P's and Q's when we communicate with them. A slight error in taste or lack of respect might end in having our heads chopped off.

One such is King Edward Theodosius the First, who resides in California and has a most delightful young secretary, Robert Mealy by name, whose calligraphy is exquisite. They paid us a visit recently, in honour of which Theodore was dubbed, and given the title of 'Right Honourable Theodore of Bull'.

All letters from His Majesty are full of pomp and circumstance and elaborately decorated with coats of arms and royal insignia. It was therefore a great relief to get permission to include in this volume extracts from our past epistolatory communications: 'We consider your most magnanimous' (actually to be truthful it was written 'magnamious') 'offer for Our Royalty to be included in your forthcoming book, why it's simply too good of you! We have been King now for nigh on eleven years but only coming out of our Minority at age Twenty-three two years ago and the 19th King of the Royal Line of Nacumeria, stretching all the way back to 724 A.D. when the ancient Duchies and Palatinates and what have you were all united by Honey the First into one solid Empire. By the way, our dating system is quite different from yours. In the usual system that you people seem to use, it would be 1424 when Honey I united the Kingdom. He died, leaving two sons, in 752.'

Nacumeria is a verdant land on the edge of the sea. It is the size of the Isle of Wight and manages to fit in quite a surprising amount of Duchies and Archimandrites. The Royal Court has public hearings every Christmas and Easter, when the Crown-wearing Ritual takes place. 'This is the time when Our Majesty dons the crown, sceptre, orb and jewelled robes. They are a bit gaudy to wear at other times.

'We are compelled to go receive our Ambassador so We must say Farewell.

'Edward Theodosius Rex I.'

Previous correspondence had only given glimpses of the pomp and grandeur surrounding His Majesty. 'Must depart. A Noble is Craving a Boon', and recently he seems to have added two more crowns to his collection by creating himself Emperor of Nargothrond and Monarch of Chubbia. According to the State Records sent by his Sec, he was 'coronated at 12.00 midnight December 31st 1974 – January 1st 1975'.

One excuse for a temporary lapse in our intercourse was that (and I quote from His Majesty again), 'I have been busy making a monetary system, writing a constitution, signing bills, figuring income-tax, balancing the budget and many other fun things like that'.

The Royal Secretary is now in his early teens, his father is Professor of Church Music at Berkeley University and the entire family provide a Royal Philharmonic Orchestra on State Occasions.

Also situated in California is another kingdom, ruled by Teddy Teeter, who has kindly issued Theodore and myself with visas in case we should choose to visit his country, which is called Stoo-Boo. I was informed by His Majesty that, whereas the U.S.A. was two hundred years old on April 14 1976, Stoo-Boo became two years old, but His Majesty was gracious enough to admit that neither fact compared with Britain's nine hundred and ten years. Our visas for Stoo-Boo will, unlike their British counterparts, not 'expire'. It says so on the form.

Alexander, King of the Royal Alexandrian Kingdom of Small Bears, lives in New Jersey and his secretary (a Miss Lydia Fillingham) graciously invited Theodore to become an Honorary Citizen of his country.

'We would like to say,' he was informed, 'that you may gain nothing monetarily or in the way of obligations but you will certainly gain in comradeship. Please sign the enclosed certificate.' Which Theodore did with his customary flourish.

From this world to a planetary one. Vikki Jane Lee possesses a Teddy who, she is convinced, comes out of the skies. The planet is Tetzlevania and the bear has informed Mrs Lee that he is the King of All the Teddies and seven thousand and eleven years old. I personally would have thought rather light ones at that. Vikki admits that he is somethimes difficult to understand because he 'lisps rather badly'. The King has a friend called Bunga Dingalong and His Majesty's name is Tetzies. He is apparently no snob because another of his close chums is Herbert Von Caravan, who is a conductor on a West Sussex bus and works on the open-air promenade deck.

King Tetzies hasn't revisited his planet recently, because, I am informed from reliable sources, they are having prune stone problems on it and prunes happen to be the National Industry there. He is therefore residing in Britain more or less incognito, only slightly disguised in a miniature Sherlock Holmes hat. Mrs Lee admits that he occasionally flies about on urgent trips with his Rocket Belt, whatever that may be.

And for human Royalists and/or Royal Family Buffs, here are the sort of facts without which no biography is complete for them. You will all be relieved to hear that there *have* been real royal Teddies. Princess Alexandra, par exemple, took it very badly when she lost hers during a goodwill tour of the Far East in

135

September 1961. Both the Burmese Army and the R.A.F. had to confess failure after massive hunts near the Irrawaddy River. There is regrettably no news of any Teddy Horses, I mean bears, owned by the Mark-Phillippses, and I don't think Prince Charles will thank me for reminding him about (a) the Teddy who accompanied him to school and (b) that 'The Teddy Bears' Picnic' was his favourite tune. On his fourth birthday a party was given for him at Buckingham Palace and the band of the Grenadier Guards played it rather a lot. It was quoted as being the most light-hearted gathering in the White and Gold Room since Queen Victoria still had children 'young enough to romp in the same spirit'.

The late Prince Tulo of Siam wisely carried his Teddy with him everywhere and popped him into a matchbox at bedtime, which I found a bit alarming but perhaps they have very big matches in Siam.

Going down just a tidge in the social scale we come to our old friend Sir Gangy de Brownman, Bt. He has been in touch with us for many years and is a great one for leaving his own visiting card all over the place when he calls. He lives in a whirl of activity and his wardrobe includes a full admiral's uniform, Regency costume for bals masqués, a hacking-jacket and a silk suit, in case he is asked to 'Buck House' as he calls the Royal London Residence. What do I mean by 'in case'? It's for *when* he is invited there.

I asked him to appear on the children's programme 'Magpie' with me some years ago when Tony Bastable was doing a feature about Teddy Bears. 'What's the rig of the day?' demanded Sir Gangy sharply. I begged him to look as smart as possible and he arrived in full Admiral's uniform, escorted by a real Admiral as it turned out. He had a huge success on the programme and I fear that Theodore's small snub nose was put enormously out of joint, not only by him, but by Mr Bastable's own bear, who was a great flying ace, called the Baron Bear Von Richthoven, of German origin, who fortunately defected to our side at a critical moment. The Baron was also in uniform festooned with medals, and there was a considerable amount of upstaging by both the distinguished warriors.

Sir Gangy, never one for not recognizing a Good Thing, is now involved deeply with North Sea Oil, and we were recently bidden to an oiling-up party in a very handsome flat overlooking Regent's Park, where Theodore and his host held court from strategic positions in a bookcase.

Another extremely influential bear in Theodore's circle of intimate friends is Harold de la Bear, who is the only member of the species who I know for certain has his name listed in a telephone directory. I say 'for certain' to forestall an avalanche of letters from angry Teddy Bear subscribers all over the globe. He is attached in a loose way to a distinguished college in Florida. He recently received his Doctorate and announced to Theodore, in a dispatch, that with this honour behind him, he was embarking on a Bear Liberation Movement which was

136

'catching on locally'. Part of the campaign was to establish Teddyphones for the members. A keen student of the theatre and indeed all the arts, he always has some trenchant statements to impart on the contemporary scene.

He is the sort of bear that Mr Souvestke, of Rockford, Virginia, is looking for. I had a rather poignant letter from him after he'd seen me on the Tom Snyder show in America. This particular chat show has a bear as mascot and the television company flew me over the Atlantic for a couple of days on condition that I brought as many teddies as I could muster. Muster! I mustered them all right! They can't wait to get their dear fat furry faces in front of the cameras.

Mr Souvestke announced that he hadn't thought of his bear for years but suddenly, on seeing the show, a traumatic childhood scene came back to him. His Teddy had been the unfortunate victim of a rainstorm and 'since I have this thing about not wanting to see poverty or harm (on persons) my parents kindly took care of the matter for me.' The purpose of his letter was to ask my advice about getting another bear. He was a writer and he seriously (and I believe him) thought that the special relationship which people and Teddies quite often have for each other might be beneficial to his work. On the other hand he didn't want just to buy one, he wanted one as a gift or one who had got lost on his travels.

The awful thing was that I didn't have one to hand which would satisfy all his requirements. He had to have a bear who would show a definite interest in the creative arts and, above all, the theatre.

'Knowing how intelligent bears are,' he wrote, 'his opinions and suggestions would be a great help. Since I write mainly comedy and about various weaknesses in the human character, the bear would have to have a sense of humour.'

I toyed with the idea of sending him Dusty but the latter had rather lost his sense of humour since the failure of *The Tiger and the Lady* and being thrown about the stage for eight perfs a week. It was out of the question to send him the original member of the cast of *Hair,* as he might be recognized going through Passport Control at Kennedy Airport. He is doubtless on the 'Wanted' list, as he was stolen in the first place and smuggled out of the country in the second. Any brouhaha might have embarrassed the waiting Mr Souvestke. I only hope that by now he has found a Teddy to suit him.

Every now and then, however, I can supply exactly what is demanded and this affords me unalloyed delight. A year or so ago a Mrs Purser sent me her old friend for safekeeping.

'Herewith,' she wrote, 'one *very* elderly Edward Bear, vintage 1904 (I think) who was my constant companion in childhood, in sickness and in health. He's rather decrepit, I am afraid, and I fully intended to repair his feet and hands (hence the small pieces of felt attached), but I lacked the courage to start on the job. So he's all yours now, if you don't think he will disgrace your collection.'

137

57 Grand Duke Ludwig of Hesse-Darmstadt with Miss Werner

56 Admiral Jetzo Hashimoto of the Imperial Japanese fleet with Herr Fritz von Katzenellenbogen of West Germany

58 King Tetzie

59 Brighteyes and Sixpence

60 Algy and friend

61 Buzzy

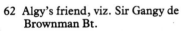

63 *Opposite:* Tony Bastable's Baron
Bear

62 Algy's friend, viz. Sir Gangy de
Brownman Bt.

von Beare

Baron Wolfgang-Manfred von Ursus-Beare flew with von Richtofen's 'Flying Circus' c. 1915. Resigned same year "through personal relationships with well-known English Bears." Left Germany via Serbia and arrived in England c. 1923. Operated ice-cream stall in Worthing c. 1928-1931. Now retired. Iron Cross IVTH Class 1912 for 'conspicuous command of a mobile bathunit in Potsdam.' Also holds Bronze Aardvark of Estonia, (with fir cones) and is Chevalier of the Golden Hive. Speaks Serbo-Croat, German, some English. Hobbies: eating, sleeping, telling anecdotes. Clubs: Honeypot, Growlers.

SOURCES: WHO'S WHO 1917.
ALMANAC DE GOTHA
IMPERIAL ARMY LIST 1916
EX-OFFICERS DEPENDENTS TRUST 1958
BASTABLE BEAR REGISTER.

She ends her letter with a sad but typical expression of regret. I say 'typical' only in the sense that it represents a situation in which I find myself involved constantly.

'It is of course quite ridiculous, but I found it hard to pack him up and part with him even now, when at seventy-one I am old enough to have got beyond this sort of thing. Maybe it's the onset of second childhood but to me he is still cuddlesome.'

Not ridiculous at all, Mrs Purser dear, and, as you know by now, there is an extremely happy sequel to your sensitive act. It so happened that a close friend of mine (and incidentally a distinguished astrologer of inestimable value to our shop and the goings-on there and Knowing What's What), was complaining constantly that I had never offered a spare bear to her to replace the loss of her childhood chum. I rather tentatively gave Mrs Sanderson (for that is our star-studier's name) the chance of securing Mrs Purser's bequest but warned her that Edward might have to undergo surgery and face a series of serious operations. Mrs S. said she didn't give a hoot, after taking one look at him, falling in love and making sure that he was a fully paid-up member of B.U.P.A.

She nursed and cossetted him for months on end and I hope that on another page you can see the electrifying results of Mrs Sanderson's loving care. She says that he even resembles her original bear and I can vouch for the remarkable similarity. When I saw an old snapshot I instinctively murmured 'Strong likeness there. First cousins at least or step-uncles, once removed.' Well the senior sitizen Edward won't ever be removed again.

Possibly the most travelled and certainly the most self-possessed Teddy Bear I have ever come across is Oliver Q. Dodger. Elsewhere you will catch glimpses of this remarkable character in exotic climes. In the 'Who's Who of the Teddy Bear World' he occupies several columns, and let me quote excerpts from that invaluable book of reference.

'Oliver Q. Dodger, born at the Spinney in Slope-on-Rye. After a quarrel with his parents, he left home at an early age and went to London to seek fame and fortune. Worked for a time as errand boy in a fashionable boutique in Carnaby Street. In the pursuit of his duties, he was unaccountably drawn to the tea-room at Selfridges, where he met a family called Batchelor. The association started uneasily because Mrs B. made some disparaging remarks about a hippy wig young Oliver had (possibly unwisely) donned for the occasion. However an honorary aunt of the Batchelors, Erin O'Hara, intervened and over a highish tea found herself inviting the bear to Germany, where they were all living at the time.

'At Buchshlag, where the senior Batchelor was stationed, he made an instant mark on the Bear Colony and became intent on furthering his career in congenial circumstances. He attended classes at a fashion school, convinced that

142

he was a Michael Fish in Embearo, but, alas and alack, he found he had no Aptitude for Design. Clever enough to relize his error, he took up ballet, but, owing to an ankle injury, he couldn't dance his way to stardom.

'It was a case of Third Time Lucky and it was in journalism that he was to find his true métier. Every well-read bear will be familiar with his acerbic but accurate comments and dispatches in *The Bearsville Courier*. This journal, it will be recalled, was originally called *The Bearsville Blah* and was run by the O'Hara sisters before being sold to a Mr Lurcher. Oliver Q. Dodger edged his way into becoming The Roving Reporter for the august paper and in this capacity travels extensively. His hobbies are listed in 'Who's Who In Bearland' as skiing, sending letters of complaint to Various Departments and Buying Clothes (for himself).

'In the pursuit of his professional duties however he is totally unselfcentred and covers the globe in search of promising material. He attended the Goldminers' Celebration in San Francisco during the Bicentennial year and was given a gold nugget to mark the occasion. In New York he took in the première of the Royal Ballet. He took part in the skiing championships in Austria and went on to Israel, as he had been commissioned to do a series on "Life In A Kibbutz". After the rigours of his time there, it was a relief to get back to the gaudy social life of Madrid and the sophistication of Paris, where he replenished his wardrobe.

'A summons from Mr Lurcher, his Editor, cut short his paid vacation and he had to race off to Berne to cover a new ballet. This aspect of his job tends to depress him somewhat as, in his own words, "Frankly, I didn't want the job of Dance Critic, but as I am the only bear on the staff who understands the Medium, I get all the assignments. But every performance I attend is poignant to me as I cannot stop thinking that, if it hadn't been for the accursed ankle, I should by now probably have my own ballet company." And doubtless he would have found room for young Michael Batchelor, currently one of the up and coming constellations in the Royal Ballet Company.

'After Berne it was a case of hot paw to view the Wagner Festspiele in Bayreuth but no sooner had Oliver started to recover from the rigours of *The Ring,* when, slightly punch-drunk, he was catapulted through the air to Zaire, to another kind of Ring, where Mohammed Ali was fighting yet one more championship.

'But the intrepid newspaper man appears to take it all in his stride and the only thing which worries his friends and admirers is his obsession with clothes. One tends to suspect that he is living slightly above his income. He recently sacked one secretary abruptly for "borrowing" his Yves St-Laurent scarf and has accepted an offer to cover the next Olympics in Moscow, solely, on dit, in order to purchase some new fur.'

What the 'Q' stands for must remain a secret, as far as we are all concerned.

Another much travelled bear, though more simply named, is John Bull, a Shropshire Lad, born in the 'Merry Thought' factory there. It says so on his foot. One day, tired of the sedentary and rather provincial life he seemed to be leading, he took a Cheap Day ticket to London to See the Sights. He never used the return half because he got a job almost immediately as a window decoration in a big London store. Here he caught the fancy of an American gentleman called Floyd Clark, who was in a wheelchair being steered by his wife, Hannetta. The couple took him back to California, where he earned good money as a sort of glorified butler to the two hundred or so bears already ensconced there.

Since her husband's death some years later, Hannetta has relied almost entirely on J.B. for company and keeping her on an even keel. They travel a lot and, apart from a penchant for touring the bars in Tangier, Mr Bull is an admirable specimen of a sensitive but sophisticated bear.

And from two globe-trotters to 'One-Eyed Connolly', who rarely sets foot outside his apartment in New York, except to travel in Mrs Helen Walton's handbag. He is her protector, her totem and, I suspect, her symbol of survival in what is essentially a tough and cruel environment. They live in a worrying neighbourhood, to put it mildly, and three times Mrs Walton has been mugged. And though the swine took money and jewellery from her bag, Connolly escaped their notice, though, as his owner wrote, 'He is far and away the most valuable thing I possess'.

A few of my ursine correspondents just want to tell me of the extraordinary things which have happened to them, like the one who was shipwrecked and spent several anxious hours in a lifeboat before being rescued and taken to Cape Town where 'I had another unpleasant experience, being severely mauled by a dog.'

One of the most fascinating bears I have had the pleasure of getting involved with was called Buzzy and was born in 1905. He belonged to the children of the British Chaplain in Bad Homburg, name of Seaton. He was a big bear and, in his early days, the children hardly played with him, as they all had small German ones to be going on with.

'Years later,' wrote Winifred Seaton, 'when we were almost grown up, Buzzy was brought out for a charade and never put away again.' Gradually he became part of the family with decided views on all family matters, smoothing over frictions as they arose. The Seaton family had by now moved to England and the rectory of a Norfolk parish. In a mysterious Honours list Buzzy was created Archdeacon of the Marshes which led to various clerical misunderstandings.

One 'incident' occurred when, for the first time ever, the Seaton family did not take the Archdeacon on holiday with them. Instead he spent the time in the house of some Roman Catholic friends, 'went over to Rome' and was promptly unfrocked on the family's return. Later he joined the Merchant Navy but, directly war was declared, he was discharged, on account of his flat feet, so he *said*.

'He is proud of the medals he won,' wrote Winifred, 'but it is hard to know *how* he won them.' Later he was forced to work again, having drawn his last National Assistance. He spent a comparatively painless week as 'a dustbin man'.

Before his eventual retirement, Winifred told me of certain physical changes that the quondam Archdeacon had had to undergo. 'A readjustment of stuffing was deemed necessary. Kapok is, I think, and always has been the chief ingredient, but he has had a number of major operations during his long life and these include not only kapok transfusions but regrafting of fur from the limbs on to the face, an entirely satisfactory operation, leaving no disfigurement at all.'

Buzzy took a sort of paternal interest in Theodore's activities. 'The Archdeacon is most sympathetic with Theodore about the Greek lessons with which he is having such difficulty. However he is a little anxious over the fast set of bears he is mixing with. Not censorious of course, remembering his own young days and particularly his hurried marriage to the charming little white bear, Julia. How grateful he was to my father,' wrote Miss Seaton, 'for performing the ceremony so that the triplets were born in wedlock, particularly as the whole affair coincided with his appointment as Archdeacon.'

Winifred died in 1973 and Mrs Morrice, a close friend of both of them sent Theodore a photograph of his illustrious counsellor, which used to repose by Miss Seaton's bedside. An accompanying note read: 'A souvenir of a *very* happy friendship.' And it has certainly been one which my tiny friend and I will always treasure.

But to end this chapter on a practical and not too soppy a note. Did you read the story of Harvey, the possum, whose mother would have nothing to do with him? Born in the Paignton Zoo in Devon, things looked very dodgy for him because, without the shelter of his mother's pouch and her daily pinta, he would have quickly died.

A substitute Mum was found for him in the shape of a Teddy Bear. Big Ted by name, belonging to the son of Jennifer Bath, the wife of the Zoo's superintendent. Jennifer simply sewed a warm flannel pouch to Ted's front and popped young Harvey inside. Then she took him home, weaned him on milk and gradually changed his diet to liquid fruit. Now he is back in the Zoo, fully equipped to face life and the gawping visitors.

We understand that Big Ted has now been put on the foster-mother rota, circulated throughout the Zoological World.

13 Theodore's chapter

After I wrote the first book some years ago there was a certain amount of criticism as to the way I had neglected Theodore. There was no picture of him, and apparently I had dismissed him with a few lines at the end of the book. In order to make amends, he is going to have an entire chapter to himself, albeit a shortish one.

At this point I am aware that I must avoid any whimsicality or saccharine sentimentality. Quite apart from you lot, he'd hate it. But, as I come to the end of this volume, I take a long long look at him. He has sat on a shelf just in front of me throughout and has given me every form of encouragement. Recently, owing to an elaborate and dangerous operation on his mouth, he has acquired a slightly less serious look on life. In fact quite often he looks as if he's sending me up.

One of his great qualities is sensibility, and I know a lot of bears who would have had their heads turned (even those who were *not* jointed) by such attention as he has received in the last decade. His television appearances on both sides of the Atlantic have resulted in a deluge of fan mail. He has had offers of marriage, and a change of home, invitations to bear house-parties and gifts galore. 'One-Eyed Connolly' gave him a sword to protect him if he *had* to go into Central Park after nightfall and might perhaps run into danger. In London he only has to carry it in Marks and Spencer during the rush hour when German tourists tend to be duelling over cardigans and cashmere sweaters.

Other acceptable items arriving from here, there and everywhere include a revolver, a grand piano which, being tone deaf like me, he generously gave to H.H. whose mastery of Bach was briefly referred to in Chapter 1, matching luggage, a brush for fur ('girls like neat bears best', the sender wrote), a great

146

deal of reading and writing material, a pair of spectacles or three, scissors, and a set of eating utensils.

A telephone arrived but I had to disconnect it after our first visit to the States when the book came out. On our return to England he kept on putting calls over the transatlantic blower to his new glamorous friends. I did however allow him to take it to France on a recent visit and you can imagine how upset he was, when we were leaving our hotel in Nîmes and couldn't find it. I stormed down to the reception desk and demanded an explanation from the concierge, who incidentally had worked with Fernandel in the early days of the latter's career and carried a photograph of them both, faded and tattered, in his inside pocket.

I explained that a telephone had disappeared and the old man looked at me as if I'd gone mad. Was it the hotel phone, he asked? No, it wasn't I replied: it belonged to my 'ours'.

I had to repeat the French for bear a great many times and the concierge then started nervously to beat a retreat from behind the counter. When I showed him Theodore in person he laughed so loudly that I doubt if even his ex-partner had ever had a similar effect on him. Theodore and I remained po-faced, natch. Eventually a maid was summoned who had to be shown Theodore. She had a similar reaction but disappeared and came back sharpish with the telephone which she *said* was under the bed.

He now has a spare one, slightly larger, presented by the Gerald Durrells, which is real bear-telephone dropping, as I happen to know that their beautiful be-spectacled bear hasn't got one in his new house at Jersey Zoo.

But to return to my relationship with Theodore. To me he is factual and as real a part of my life as anything I possess. He doesn't remotely resemble a favourite tie, watch or any inanimate object. As far as I'm concerned I wouldn't compare him with a cat or dog but I'll tell you something. I would no more dream of going away without him, even for a night, than flying to the moon. But then I've never really fancied *that*, though I think Theodore, being more adventurous than I, might rather like it. He was quite jealous of that one who did go up with that astronaut, a gift from his daughter.

Yet I know that the same thing would happen on the moon as it does in New York, Greece, Hollywood or Moreton-in-Marsh: i.e. the moment I unpack and put Theodore beside my bed, the strange place becomes a sort of home. I suppose he's a symbol of unloneliness. He sits there on his haunches (how he *hates* standing up!) reminding me of the happy and unhappy times we've had together, and his funny little face and outstretched paws give me a lift when things are looking a bit bleak.

At this very moment of typing he is pretending to study a tiny Greek-English lexicon which I gave him hopefully. Perhaps he'll look up 'bleak'.

I imagine that if my mother *hadn't* given away my original Teddy to the jumble sale, he wouldn't be here at all. In Greece I mean. He'd be sitting on the mantelpiece in my flat in London, feeling sad and neglected. He wouldn't be lonely because he would be surrounded by a complete glass menagerie of tiny animals, people and vehicles which I have accumulated over the years (65). But I wouldn't have felt the same about the entire Teddy Bear species if it hadn't been for the deprivation of a bear who would probably have been too heavy to cart everywhere at my time of life, to say nothing of the possible overweight involved on the plane.

Though recently a twenty-five-year-old actress left London Airport for New York, clutching her Teddy, which cost her just the fifty dollars in excess baggage, and an English girl, having forgotten to bring hers, paid £9 (it would be £15 at least by now) to have him shipped over later.

Luckily Theodore is pretty mobile with his two-and-a-half-inch body and can easily be slipped into a pocket. He also has his own passport (another of One-Eyed Connolly's Useful and Acceptable Gifts) which avoids any ranagazoo at frontiers.

Although I haven't, I hope, been nauseatingly sloppy about Theodore I can fully sympathize with people who go overboard about their friends. The one indisputably healthy thing which has emerged out of all this rummaging in the cupboards of the Teddy Bear world has been that hundreds of people are now less cautious of expressing emotions which they might have thought would be construed as childish.

In this they confuse the word 'childish' with 'childlike', an entirely different thing and surely one of the most endearing of qualities. And age simply doesn't enter into it. The older the friend, the more he is valued. Particularly when that friend shows the characteristics which can cement a relationship so strongly. One only has to look at a genuine Teddy's face to see at once the loyalty, dependability and, above all, understanding behind it. They are, let us face it, the best *listeners* in the world.

Theodore has friends all over the world and he deals with some of his correspondents in, what seems to me, rather a peremptory fashion. Honey, a rag doll of doubtful parentage, wrote to him to report that her mistress sings to her and lulls her to sleep.

'Does your master sing or read to you?' she asked Theodore.

'No, thank God,' he replied.

Another regular Pen Pal is Miss Ophelia Bear, whose owner is always having emotional problems. Currently she is in love with a middle-aged doctor who won't marry her because he thinks he is too old.

'Paula is very unhappy,' wrote Miss O. Bear. 'Sometimes I get all wet from her holding me close and crying. I don't think that difference in age is all that important, do you?'

148

64 Theodore tries to work out his destiny

'No,' wrote Theodore, though secretly terrified at what all this was leading up to.

When Colonel Henderson and I finally get around to holding the Greatest Teddy Bear Picnic of All Time, I'm willing to bet that the average age of those attending will be nearer forty than fourteen. It was the Colonel who originally suggested that 'we should have a rally for the little chaps'. I concurred enthusiastically and haven't done a sausage about it. The terrible thing was that it leaked out to the Press that such an event was in the melting pot, and we had enquiries from all over the globe from people who wanted to attend such a function, with their friends of course.

But it will take place somehow, somewhere, some time. The Royal Albert Hall in London and Madison Square in New York immediately leap to mind as possible venues. Will they be too large, we ask ourselves? *No*, cry the Colonel and I. We don't think we should charge an entrance fee ('everyone just bring their own Ted' suggests the Colonel) but we would have to flog the event to television companies and/or film dittos so that we could at least cover expenses.

The whole prospect is pretty heady stuff. Shall we be fortunate enough to see some of the all time greats of the Teddy Bear World gathered together under one roof? Will the heroic bears like Mr Woppit and the one who climbed the Matterhorn be able to make it? Can we ensure that Archibald Ormsby-Gore and Oliver Q. Dodger honour us with their presence? Will the real Pooh suddenly make an appearance and above all will the Original Teddy, now in the Smithsonian Museum, under guard in a glass case and I think an *imposter* (only fifty years old if he's a day) will he step forward, prove that he is Anastasia, I mean The Original Teddy, as the Surprise Item of the Rally?

In any event the turn-out will be fantastic. You will all see (if you come) the Teddies who have survived earthquakes, floods, fires, broken homes, hospitals, and bombs, to say nothing of those who are short on fur, eyes, ears and limbs. But in their battered faces you will be able still to recognize the indefinable magic quality which has made the Teddy Bear so unique a figure throughout the twentieth century.

It must be admitted however that not everybody is as devoted to the subject as Colonel H. and myself. When I first started on the research, I received a postcard from a gentleman I had been led to believe would spill some bear beans of great interest to us all:

'Dear Mr Bull,' it read, 'I regret that I have no son with valuable information on the Teddy Bear subject. My boys have very little information on any subject. I do have a rather curious aunt in Savannah who has sent you my name. Anytime you do a symposium on curious aunts I should be glad to help.'

150

Appendix

Those bears having trouble with the above or other parts of their anatomy should get in touch with one or other of the following hospitals or nursing homes which specialize in this sort of problem.

('Teddy, having met up with a rather unfriendly Collie Dog, is in desperate need of a reputable surgeon. Could you please recommend one?' is typical of the sort of SOS I get.)

Great Britain

The Dolls Hospital
16 Dawes Road
London SW6
385 2081

Mrs Denton Rich
'Saddlers'
Sandy
Bedfordshire
Sandy 80668

Mrs Wallace-Jeffries
Waterhead House
The Banks
Seascale
Cumbria CA20 1QP

H. Howard Shepherd
5 Pafford Avenue
Watcombe
Torquay
S. Devon T22 8BS
(Mr Shepherd will also take care of old Teddies or homeless dittoes)

Mrs Clare Dodds
Lookout Garden Flat
3 Marine Hill
Clevedon
Avon BS21 7PW

Minutiques (Props. J. and C. Jackman)
82b Trafalgar Street
Brighton BN1 4EB
Brighton 681862 (day), 551042 (evening)

USA

The Dolls Hospital
787 Lexington Avenue
New York 10021
838 7527

The Grizzlies
Mesdames Lowery and Hixson
223 W. Lloyd Street
Pensacola
Florida 32501
904-434 0006 904-432 8803

Homes for retired and/or elderly bears
Mr Shepherd (see previous page) will care for old Teddies or homeless dittoes with great pleasure.

In Ivy, Virginia, in the United States, there is a similar establishment run by Mrs Iris Carter, who has flatteringly named her Teddy Bear Museum after me. All visitors are welcome, and so are elderly and notable Teddies. One lady dispatched her friend with a silk scarf around his neck with 'a darling brooch' and a note: 'Please given Wilbur a good home'. Another contributor said she would send Mrs Carter her bear if she was also willing to take her Buster Brown and an elephant 'as she didn't want to break up the family'. A seventy-year-old gentleman said he had had his bear since childhood and would be willing to trade him for some antique marbles. 'Don't send money,' he wrote, 'I don't need it.' Mrs Carter had to break it to him that she didn't have any marbles, but ten days later he sent the bear anyway.

Additional Bear Information
Particularly distinguished members of the species can be visited at the following museums:

In London: The Bethnal Green Museum, Cambridge Heath Road, E2.
980 3024 980 4315
Pollock's Toy Museum, 1 Scala Street, W1
636 3452

In Brighton: The National Toy Museum, The Royal Pavilion, Art Gallery and Museums, Brighton. Part of the collection is on view at the Grange, Rottingdean.

In Worthing: The Worthing Museum.

In Edinburgh: The Museum of Childhood, 38 Hight Street, Edinburgh.

152

A Private Collection can be viewed by writing to:
  Mrs Helen Mackinnon or her daughter Deidre,
  Silvertrees,
  Scamill,
  West Kilbride,
  Ayrshire,
  Scotland.

Some emporia at which bears can view prospective owners
Harrods. Hamleys. Orsis in Knightsbridge Green. Hummel in the Burlington
Arcade. Tiger Tiger and Laffeaty's both in King's Road. Homebound
Craftsmen at 25A Holland Street, W8. In New York the agents for Steiff Bears
are F.A & O. Schwartz on Fifth Avenue.

The Good Bears of the World Association
Inspired by Russell McLean's efforts in America, this excellent organisation was
inaugurated in 1973. Its principal aims are to encourage affection towards
children, especially ailing children, and to provide Teddy Bears for them in
hospital and institutions where the need is greatest.

   Colonel Bob Henderson has undertaken the leadership of the Association in
the United Kingdom. His untiring work for Friends of the Bear (to say nothing
of the Bears themselves) is truly beyond praise.

   During the last few years this organisation has made remarkable progress on
both sides of the Atlantic. A well-known broadcaster and journalist, Jim Ownby,
started things going the other side of the Atlantic and dens have sprung up from
Hawaii to High Wycombe, and many hospitals have benefitted from this
activity.

   Naturally, this charitable work needs funds to continue this good service, so
there is a nominal subscription to the Good Bears of the World for membership.
For further particulars you should write, enclosing a stamped addressed
envelope, to:
  GBW (UK)
  17 Barnton Gardens
  Edinburgh EH4 6AF
  Scotland

   If you decide to become a member, and Theodore and I cannot recommend
such action too highly, you will receive a copy of 'Bear Tracks', a riveting
newsletter crammed with Bear News Items from all over the world. This
publication appears several times a year.